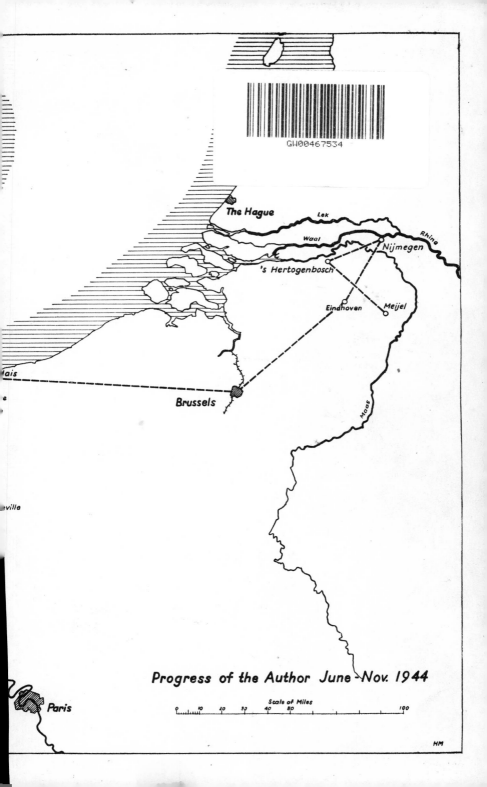

The Hague

Lek

Waal

Rhine

Nijmegen

's Hertogenbosch

Eindhoven

Meijel

Maas

ais

Brussels

ville

Paris

Progress of the Author June - Nov. 1944

Scale of Miles

0   10   20   30   40   50   100

HM

Normandy: Crocodiles flaming enemy in a farm.

FLAME THROWER

by

ANDREW WILSON

Formerly Captain, M.C., The Buffs

WILLIAM KIMBER

LONDON

Published by

WILLIAM KIMBER AND CO. LIMITED

100 Jermyn Street, London SW1Y 6EE

© Andrew Wilson 1956 and 1984
ISBN 0-7183-0522-1

First Published 1956
This edition reprinted 1984

PRINTED IN GREAT BRITAIN BY BIDDLES LIMITED
GUILDFORD AND KING'S LYNN

CONTENTS

ILLUSTRATIONS

All the above photographs are reproduced by kind permission of the Imperial War Museum.

AUTHOR'S NOTE TO THE FIRST EDITION

The events in this story happened between 1943 and 1945 in the 141st Regiment, Royal Armoured Corps (The Buffs). I believe that my feelings and experiences were not very different from those of many other young officers in a flame-thrower unit—except that for some the experiences were more unpleasant. For this reason, and because of a feeling of detachment which comes from describing what happened eleven years ago, I have found it easier to write in the third person.

INTRODUCTION

I
T is nearly forty years since the events in this book
happened, and thirty since I wrote about them—naively,
but with near-total recall. They were still so close then that
I felt I could write only in the third person. I even used false
names until persuaded to put in the real ones by my
publisher. In this new (fifth) edition I wondered whether to
revert to the simple "I", since I am no longer inhibited from
speaking directly about what I experienced; but I finally
decided that, rather than tinker with what I had written, almost
literally with blood, in an attempt to get the war out of my
system, I would add a short introduction and try to say some of
the things I could not perceive at the time.

The fighting in Normandy and later in Holland and
Germany was by no means the bloodiest part of the war. (One
has only to look at the savagery on the Russian front or in the
Pacific.) But it was bad enough to be branded on the memory of
anyone who took part. My own experience was dominated by
the weapon issued to the regiment in which I was a
twenty-year-old lieutenant. The Crocodile flame-thrower was
unlike any previous kind of flame-thrower. It had been
developed in 1942-3 as a "secret-weapon"—one of several to be
taken into action by Maj.-Gen. Hobart's 79th Armoured
Division.

The flame-projector was mounted in the front of a Churchill
Mark VII tank, where the flame-gunner sat beside the

driver. The turret of the tank contained the usual Churchill armament, a 75mm cannon and a co-axially mounted machine-gun. Four hundred gallons of heavy, viscous flame fuel were carried in a seven-ton trailer connected to the tank by an armoured link containing the fuel pipe. The liquid was protected from the nozzle of the gun under pressure of nitrogen at 350 lb per square inch. This had been reduced from 5,000 lb per square inch in the five long steel cylinders or "bottles" in which the nitrogen was stored in the trailer. The rod of fuel was ignited by a jet of burning petrol that had passed over two electrodes. The gun had a range of about ninety yards and, if operated continuously, could flame for about two minutes.

The Crocodile was intended to be used against German gun emplacements on the Normandy beaches. But after D-Day it became a battlefield terror weapon for use against enemy positions of all kinds It was widely believed that its fearsome appearance in action would cause enemy troops to abandon their positions. This sometimes happened. But there were often circumstances in which positions could not be abandoned, or when individuals, especially wounded, were trapped. The results were then terrible.

As the book tells, it was some time before I became properly aware of this. Even when I did so, the emotions I felt were swamped by the totality of feelings to which everyone is subject in war, above all awareness of the uncertainty of one's survival and fear of disgracing oneself or "letting down the side".

From time to time attempts have been made to outlaw incendiary weapons (of which Crocodiles were one) by international agreement. The campaign gained strength with the use of napalm in Korea and then Vietnam. The fuel used by the Crocodile—a mixture of petrol, naphtha and rubber—was a crude form of napalm before the name was invented. It is therefore arguable that flame-throwers should also be proscribed. But legal opinion is against it. This is because the chief humanitarian objection to air-dropped napalm in Vietnam was its failure to discriminate between combatants and civilians, whereas flame-throwers are no more indiscriminate than artillery shells.

(There is also another objection. If war were sufficiently "cleaned up", rulers would have even fewer scruples about resorting to it.)

Yet to have commanded a troop of flame-throwing tanks can cause one reflections that need not affect gunners, whose job, like that of bomber crews, normally precludes immediate confrontation with the result of their handiwork. Long after *Flame Thrower* was written, I was invited, as defence correspondent for my newspaper, to make a short voyage aboard a Polaris submarine. During that exercise I was reminded of something I say in the book about the contrast between the technical elegance of modern weapons and the ugly reality of their effects. Faced with Polaris, I was struck by the contrast between nuclear devastation and the sixteen missiles in their gleaming white launch tubes. With the Crocodile it was the contrast between my first sight of charred bodies and the neat working diagrams by means of which we had been introduced to the flame-thrower during training.

Recently my eye was caught by a bookseller's window containing a book with a glossy cover picture of a Churchill Mark VII Crocodile in immaculate camouflage paint. I have long been puzzled by the cult of the military that manifests itself in coffee-table books of World War II hardware. I wanted to go into the shop and put beside it a picture of a trench a Crocodile had flamed, or the interior of a Crocodile that had been penetrated by a German eighty-eight. At least it would have been a healthier memento.

My war generation was very young. The average age of tank

crews in my regiment was twenty-two; many were still in their teens. My sergeant, Warner, who died at Rosmalen was twenty. Forty years later, whenever I think of the war, my world is still populated by twenty-year-olds. I cannot imagine that any of us has changed. This has a bizarre consequence. Whenever, in the course of my work, I have to visit the Ministry of Defence, I find it strange to be talking to middle-aged generals who, unlike us youngsters, have never seen a real war.

The fact is, we were not just fighting. We were also growing up. At least I was. A young officer with no experience of life beyond a pre-war public school and an officer cadet training unit was condemned to a peculiarly English prolongation of adolescence. All that I needed to learn about life, all that my school had not taught me, I learned from members of my crew. My education ranged from a fine new Anglo-Saxon vocabulary to how not to get a girl pregnant. It also endowed me with a lasting scorn of social hierarchies. At the same time the sharing of danger created a comradeship that was going to be difficult ever to find again. Certainly I myself never found it, though I must have spent a lifetime looking.

Our extreme youth—one could almost say virginity in the case of most junior officers—is one reason why I shall always wince at the *machismo* with which the facts of war are generally dressed up by film makers and others. Certainly there can never have been a less "macho" army than the plodding Welsh and English infantry I was assigned to support in Normandy that summer, or our own selves preoccupied with the performance of our complex and horrible machines.

A lot of pious nonsense has been written about courage in war. Books are expected to focus on it, notwithstanding the fact that so much of what passes for courage is the product of accident, or lack of imagination. I certainly witnessed acts of physical courage on the battlefield—generally in conditions of obscurity, in the confusion of artillery bombardments or in darkness on minefields. (Two of my friends were killed attempting to rescue comrades on booby-trapped minefields.) But the bravest act by any member of my regiment was a moral one—the attempt by William Douglas Home to arrange an unauthorised cease-fire at Le Havre, for which he was court-martialled, cashiered and sent to prison.

Even more nonsense has been written and spoken about patriotism. Any notion that we were fighting for our country, or to free Europe from Hitler, or to make a better world, is largely romantic. We were fighting in order to stay alive, and our loyalties were not to our country, not to our service, not to our regiment even, but intensely to one another—within the twenty-strong troop or, on occasion, the squadron. Nor do I find anything belittling in this realisation. For, as I have said, it was for most of us the first, and unrepeatable, experience of escaping from our narrow selves.

I must have decided long ago, probably about the time I started writing *Flame Thrower*, that this memory of the real world of my youth was unlikely to survive contact with the latter-day, grown-up personifications of the men I had known so closely in 1944-5. Of course, we meet from time to time, some of us—and with foreknowledge of failure attempt to bridge the unbridgeable, recalling trivialities, exchanging ritual jokes. But we are middle-aged strangers to one another. Our whole conversation is a fruitless attempt to deny this.

And yet, surely, we have the same thoughts. Do they not sometimes wake up in the middle of the night as I do, and, ignoring the comfort of a soft bed and secure walls, reach out to recall the precise feel of the gun barrel one gripped, and the position of the towing bracket on which one placed a foot, in order to mount the tank before taking it into action? Do they not carry in their minds the same unfaded pictures—in Normandy of white-dusted fields, fire-reddened tank hulls, the grotesquely bent dead beneath the apple blossom; in Holland of burned villages with their pungent evening peat-smell, the huge steel bridges rising high above the mist on the mined and mortared polder?

There are moments when the memory of these things is almost unbearable. How can it have been so real then, and be so remote now? What was the meaning of it, this second of history overshadowing our whole lives? With whom can one share the knowledge of what it was really like?

The answer is no one. For we all died forty years ago.

February 1984

I

THE REGIMENT

IT started for different people at different times, and for Wilson it started on the square at Sandhurst on the last Friday in February, 1943. The other squads were standing at attention down three long sides of it. On the steps of the Old Building there was a flash of red. The general was moving over to take the salute.

"Passing-out Troops, inward—turn! By the centre, slow —march!"

The band struck up "Auld Lang Syne". The two lines wheeled into each other. Up towards the steps they went, following the movement of the march; check, forward, check, forward . . . out of the clear, sad winter afternoon, up the steps and under the Georgian portico.

Inside the building with its musty smell of central heating there was no "dismiss": they just melted away, running down the strangely empty corridors. Wilson heard the clatter of the Adjutant's horse as it followed the last file into the vestibule. There was little Bishop in front. Would you ever see him again? And Wright, still green from last night's party. It wasn't war. It was breaking up school.

Or was it?

Suddenly Wilson remembered his old anxiety. Would he be in time for the invasion?

For the past two years the invasion had dominated his life. The rest of the war—in Africa, Burma, the Pacific—

was a side-show. He had thought about the invasion even in
1940, watching the German Heinkels swarm in from the
Channel, and again when he slipped away from school and
into the recruiting office. He had even remembered it in the
long, dreary year with the young soldiers' battalion, waiting
for an O.C.T.U. board and the chance to get to a tank
regiment.

He had no idea when the invasion was going to be, but
now at least he would make it. He was just nineteen.

He spent his passing-out leave with his parents at their
home by the sea in Kent. His father had lost an arm and the
sight of an eye, when he led a patrol in German East Africa
in 1917. His mother had nursed him through the years of
pain and distress which followed. War had twisted and
ruined their lives; but they didn't mention it. They accepted
the new war—as they had accepted the old—with un-
questioning patriotism.

There was someone else who did that—and that was his
father's old Commanding Officer, Colonel Barton. The
colonel lived in a big house in the country, with an old soldier
to look after him. The walls of the drawing-room were
covered with faded photographs of regimental groups and
cases of medals won by his regiment in Africa and India.
He had bought them out of pawn shops; and when he died
he would give them to the regiment, along with his own
decorations.

Wilson went to see him. He wanted to thank him for the
letter he had written to help him get his posting. It was
terribly important to get to a good regiment—and the one
he was going to had the proudest tradition of any of the
Line. Looking into the old man's eyes as he said goodbye,
Wilson resolved to do the regiment credit.

Two days later the shabby war-time train clanked and

clattered into Ashford station. He put on his greatcoat with its new gilded stars and picked up his cane and gloves. A goods shed swung by, the beginning of a platform, a scattering of khaki and civilian figures. There was excitement on this strange sunlit platform as he pushed his way through the crowd to the guard's van. Then suddenly the crowd parted and a captain was coming towards him.

"Wilson?"

With a jerk he remembered that one didn't salute captains now. "Yes."

"My name's Hayward. How do you do? Where are your things?"

They drove out of the Sunday-sleepy town and up through Kentish lanes.

"You've come at an odd time," said the captain. "The regiment's out on a scheme till Tuesday." He was aloof after his first greeting.

The regiment was stationed in a big park with its headquarters in the pseudo-Tudor mansion. Wilson spent his first day wandering round the lines; the rows of tarred Nissen huts, each with fourteen beds, a cheerless empty stove and a swept concrete floor. The paths between huts were edged with whitewashed stones and everywhere there were patterns of stones with the regimental crest.

That evening he sat in the ante-room of the mess, in his stiff new service dress, waiting for supper. The silver and trophies were stored away, but dividing the ante-room from the mess itself was a big plaster-board screen with a hideous picture of a Churchill tank spitting bullets at a handful of cringing Germans.

"Makes the room, doesn't it?" said Harry Barrow.

Harry was one of the few officers who had not gone out on the scheme—he, and Captain Hayward and a major. "Well," he had said when he introduced himself, "I'm not one of you posh bastards, but I'll stand you a beer." After a while he began to talk about training. Wilson took his chance. "When do you expect to go overseas?" he said.

"Overseas?" roared Harry. "This lot? Frig me, we'll be lucky if they'll have us in the army of occupation."

That evening there was an ENSA show.

"Coming?" said the major. He was gruff but not unfriendly.

They all went to the NAAFI, where the chairs were arranged in rows with armchairs for the officers. It was freezing outside and there was only a little coke stove.

"All right to begin, sir?"

A little comic's face, its nose red with grease paint, nodded and withdrew behind the curtain, followed by the cheers and claps and catcalls of the troops. Then from behind the curtain came a long tormented wail.

"Christ, what's that?" said Barrow.

"The Lomond Girl Pipers," said the major flatly.

The curtain opened uncertainly and there stood the pipers, mother and daughter, marking time with high-raised knees. For minutes the music was lost in a renewed outburst of cheers and clapping. Then with blown-out cheeks and a look of determination they made figures of eight. The music died without warning. They came to attention side by side.

"Encore," shouted a corporal, when the cheers died down. But the next turn was the comic.

"You know, boys, coming here tonight we lost our way, so down in Ashford I stopped and asked a girl. . . ." Harry Barrow leaned across: "A bloke told the same one last time."

The joke moved on excruciatingly to its big moment, something about a squadron sergeant-major. There was a little desultory tittering.

14

The comic tried half a dozen others, all local colour stuff, but the other man had used up almost everything.

Finally he bowed himself off. The troops clapped uproariously, perhaps to show they admired spirit.

The pipers reappeared, this time in tights. Wilson could see the goose-pimples on their cold thighs.

"Queenie, the queen of the burlesque show," they sang in unison. ". . . and she stops," sang the daughter. "But only just in time."

"Take 'em off," shouted the troops, joining in the chorus.

Barrow nudged Wilson's arm. "I could do with the little one."

But up in the mess, when the show was over, it was Wilson the little one liked. She eyed him from two feet away, across a collection of empty whisky glasses. On the other side of the room he heard the comic: "With a little show like this, you've got to give the boys something. Now I could name you plenty of 'A' shows, where they don't do more than a five-minute number apiece . . ."

The waiter brought more whiskies, lots more whiskies, and suddenly the major was dancing with the mother. "Come on," he said, "join in." Wilson got up to dance. But next moment he fell down on a chair, the daughter on top of him. Her wet lips were only a few inches away. All at once the major was standing over them.

"Go and kiss the bloody girl," he roared.

Wilson shut his eyes and obeyed.

Next morning the rest of the regiment came back and everything was different. Wilson had to report to the C.O.

The C.O. looked at him, summing him up. He wore 1914–18 medal ribbons on his ill-fitting battle-dress. His cuffs were too short and the trouserlegs just above his gaiters refused to lie down in the intended plus-fours fashion.

15

"Do you know anything about Bren-gun carriers?"

"Yes, sir."

Pause.

"You'd better go with the reconnaissance troop."

As Wilson was about to go the C.O. leaned forward to shake hands. It was the only time that Wilson ever came into close contact with him.

For the next three months he spent every day in the tank park, where the subalterns stood about in their overalls watching the men work. Wherever they went they carried their little leather canes. It was an offence to be without a cane. In the evening everyone came back, the men to their dreary huts, the officers to the mess.

It was a serious, dignified mess now. The subalterns had to be in the ante-room half an hour before dinner; they sipped weak beer and queued up to use the undersized billiard table. The majors and captains came later and stood at the other end of the room. There was no smoking for half an hour before dinner.

Wilson tried to pick out the people he liked. Apart from the other subalterns, who were forced into a sort of proletarian camaraderie, there was the gentle Squadron Commander of Headquarters, Major Edmeades. He looked a cross between a classics don and a civil engineer. The men called him "Steady Eddy".

Then there was Drysdale, the R.E.M.E. officer, who, because he wore a different badge, felt free to talk with the untouchables and even to sit among them at table; and Dixie Dean, the chubby little captain from "B" Squadron, who was always being cheeky to the Second-in-Command.

Finally there was William Douglas Home, the second captain of "C", who would stand warming his tall, insolent body in front of the fire and say, as he raised his whisky

16

glass: "My ambition, Colonel, is to continue and end the war like this." He couldn't mean it, of course.

One day in the tank park, Wilson was talking to the lieutenant who looked after the headquarters tanks—the tanks the C.O. and the Adjutant were supposed to use in battle. His name was Harvey, and Wilson called him "Pooh", because he looked like a big, good-natured bear. A little way off the men were getting the vehicles ready for the Friday inspection.

"Don't the tanks ever go out?" said Wilson.

"Of course not. They're non-runners most of the time."

"How's that?"

"Haven't you ever heard of over-maintenance," said Pooh. "Every week we do our weekly maintenance; and the handbook says 'Once a week, check nuts and unions'. Well, every time a driver checks a nut, he pulls it a fraction tighter. After he's done that about sixteen weeks running, the nut shears off. Then he has to wait for a new part."

All the same, there was another scheme at the beginning of summer, and thirty tanks were runners out of fifty-four. They rolled out of camp one fine May morning towards the open downs. Not more than a third broke down, most of them near roadside cafés.

On the third day of the scheme, a senior officer of the regiment sent Wilson and a section of carriers to do a reconnaissance. They raced through a field of young wheat and threw some thunderflashes at a posse of Canadians brewing coffee. Then they raced back and reported. The officer was standing in a ditch, his under-sized helmet perched ridiculously forward on his forehead.

"Well," he said. "Is it held?"

"Yes," said Wilson.

Just then a smouldering thunderflash landed and exploded between the officer's legs, but he continued to pore over his map.

On the way back to camp Wilson heard the "ghost voice". The officer commanding the column had been talking to the regiment over the wireless. It had rained for the last two days, and he was trying to tell the men that he appreciated their spirit. It took a long time, like a B.B.C. news broadcast.

"You have just heard the news, and that was so-and-so reading it," said a voice on the net. Suddenly the air was painfully empty. Wilson waited for a disciplinary explosion. Surely they'd stop the column and find the culprit. But nothing happened.

"It goes on all the time," said Harvey, as they walked to the mess beneath the dripping trees. "It could be anyone in the sergeants' or corporals' crews."

On his first leave from the regiment Wilson went to see Colonel Barton again. He felt guilty for not having written to him.

"Reconnaissance, eh?" said the colonel. His eyes lit up and immediately Wilson saw dancing there some picture of bygone patrols in India or Africa. "Reconnaissance," he repeated, "you can use initiative in a job like that!"

A moment later the manservant brought in the tea—a frugal tea with thinly buttered bread, for the colonel was punctilious about rationing.

As soon as it was laid, the colonel got up and went to the big oak cupboard, where he kept his diaries and other treasures. Presently he came back with a book and a leather case in his hand.

"Look, I don't suppose I'll be needing these again."

He handed Wilson first the book, a squat little textbook, *Mounted Reconnaissance* (1912), with faded khaki covers and inside the cover in copperplate handwriting, "C. W. Barton, 2nd Battn. Royal —— Regiment."

"I know things have changed, of course; but the principles are the same, aren't they?"

"Yes, indeed, sir," said Wilson; but his eyes were already fixed on the shiny calf-skin case, whose strap the colonel was undoing. He took out a pair of field-glasses.

They were terrific—Zeiss X6. The black enamel on the rims had worn down to the brass. But the lenses were like crystal.

"Look after them," said the colonel. "They were a present from my father. I used them at Ladysmith."

On the last night of leave, when he packed his valise, Wilson put the glasses in the centre, so they wouldn't be damaged.

"Aren't you taking this?" said his mother. She held up *Mounted Reconnaissance*.

"Not this time."

"And this?"

"Yes, I'm taking that. I'd almost forgotten it," he said. And she handed him his Bible.

When he got back to the regiment Wilson made up his mind to ask for a transfer from Reconnaissance. But various things intervened.

"You're down to go on a battle course," said Harvey.

"Why me?" said Wilson.

"Everyone's got to go. We've been put in Second Army."

"What does that mean?"

"Christ knows."

In the mess Harry Barrow stood him a whisky. "Ten per cent casualties at battle school," he said.

Darlington at five in the morning. Coffee from the W.V.S. The local train chugged out to the moors. Some of the others must have been going to battle school; but no one talked. They slept unshaven in the corners of the cold compartment, till a voice shouted "Barnard Castle!" It was only October, but the trucks which were to take them from the station were powdered with snow.

There were comfortable dormitories and scalding-hot showers and a hearty recreation room at the school. "But why all Scots instructors?" asked a depressed little subaltern with a Home Counties regiment shoulder-flash.

Wilson was put in a squad with twenty others. The first day they paraded on the square and someone in the rear rank accidentally let off a Bren gun. They carried off the little man from the Home Counties regiment.

"Only a nick in the arse," said the Black Watch instructor cheerfully.

Next day they took out some carriers and went up into the high moors, where the snow was three inches deep.

"We're going to do a carrier assault on trenches," said the instructor. He led off a section and showed them. "Now you do it."

He handed over the carrier to a young Guards ensign, a fresh-faced boy in a dark-brown tailored battle-dress. The ensign climbed in and tapped the driver's shoulder.

The carrier leapt forward across the rough ground. Half-way to the target he rested the gun on the side of the carrier and fired. But something went wrong. Suddenly the ensign wasn't to be seen any more. The gun went on firing, out of sight and curiously muffled—all thirty rounds.

The driver stopped and waved his arms. The instructor dashed over.

"The gun must have slipped inside when we went over a bump," said the driver. "He couldn't stop firing."

The ensign's finger was jammed against the trigger. The Bren had emptied nearly its whole magazine against the inside of the armour, a few inches from his face.

When they lifted him out, his battle-dress had dark damp patches, which gave it a rust colour; there were raw red gashes where his eyes had been.

"Where's that bloody ambulance?"

It had stood by all the time; but now they couldn't get it through the snow. Orderlies made up a stretcher and carried the ensign away.

The squad went on training. "You've got to master your weapons," said the instructor.

In the next three weeks they were put through the "tough" things. Clawing through wire with a machine-gun firing a couple of feet above their heads. Crawling upside down along a seemingly endless pole of scaffolding, while instructors threw sticks of gelignite. Panting uphill with bursting eardrums and thumping hearts to lunge with bayonets at straw-filled sacks. Bursting through the "haunted house" with tommy-guns blazing at dummy figures which sprang without warning from doorways and floors and ceilings.

The Scots instructors loved the pipes. Once, when the squad had scrambled up a waterfall, blinded and sick with exertion, an exotically tartaned figure emerged from the moss and bracken playing a lament. Another time they did an assault seventy-five yards behind a creeping artillery barrage, with three stalwart Cameronians playing "The Cock o' the North".

"The pipes are a fine, steadying influence," said one of the instructors.

"Steadying, my arse," said a wiry Welshman as he dug a twenty-five pounder nosecap from the mess-tins in his haversack.

Yet, curiously, there were no more casualties.

Back at the regiment something had happened. Wilson knew it at once when the station wagon whisked him past the tank park. The tank park was empty.

"The C.O.'s gone," said Harvey. On the colonel's last night the captains and majors had given an enormous party and thrown him through the screen with the picture of the Churchill.

Momentarily, inexplicably, Wilson felt regret. It must be hard to lose one's regiment, and according to his lights he'd done his duty. Wireless and the petrol engine killed him. In the earlier war he was probably a first-class officer.

"Who's the new man?"

"A Scotsman—Highland Light Infantry."

"When does he come?"

"Next week."

Colonel Waddell had slightly bandy legs, and his stocky body was perpetually hunched forward, as if pressing up into an invisible rugger scrum. His face was enormous, roughened and creased. He had ice-blue eyes, and his mat of copper hair seemed half a size too small for him.

"D'ye find yourself constipated, Wilson?"

He had scarcely arrived, and already they had moved out of the mess and were camping on the training area for a two-day exercise. Sitting on the officers' latrine, the new C.O. probed Wilson for his opinion of the temporary diet of biscuits. He asked about everything. At any moment he would swoop on a scared trooper or subaltern and stun him with questions about the condition of his stomach, feet, gun, tank, wife, morals or religion. Equally often he would cut across the mess, where "shop" was forbidden, and hold down a major to discuss the rôle of armour in a break-through.

He had been a peace-time stockbroker, a territorial. Soon, when he came into the mess, some officers of the "Old Guard" began to keep their backs turned. Undaunted, he would tap their backs and produce the next week's training programme. It was plain that between the C.O. and the court of his predecessor a bitter, unspoken conflict was developing. Yet the outcome was never in doubt. Waddell was supported by the powers which mattered.

After Waddell's arrival there were still the weekly inspections of tanks and lines. But they were very different now. Instead of searching the vehicles for specks of mud, the C.O. would climb aboard and ask the driver to start up; or would order the gunner to produce the spare firing-pin of the six-pounder. Up in the lines a few nervous officers would still order new coats of paint for the fire-buckets. But Waddell didn't notice these things. He wanted to know why the coal for the stoves was so poor.

Wilson had a tank troop at last—three Churchills, each with a crew of five—in "A" squadron. But it wasn't an easy troop.

The men were discontented, sometimes almost mutinous. They were caught in a fork. On one hand the C.O.'s probing, his constant demand for efficiency. On the other, the hang-over of the old regime—the constant fatigues for cook-house, salvage and hut-sweeping, which took two thirds of them away from their tanks and training each day.

"Wilson!"

He was doing the rounds of Orderly Officer, when Waddell trapped him.

23

"Wilson, I've a job for ye. I've been thinking ye'd make a good entertainments officer."

Waddell, searching for resources in his lonely struggle with men and officers, had dug into the question of regimental funds—the money coming from the profit on dry buns and watery tea in the NAAFI. It was there to be used for the men's welfare. But the old colonel had been keen to present a "healthy balance sheet". The money had been left to accumulate, except for some outlay on items like paint for inspections and an unofficial silvered cap badge for the men.

"There's near on a thousand pounds in P.R.I. account. Ye're going to help liquidate it. Go and see Major Duffy."

Like most of the other subalterns, stretched and ground in the regimental upheaval, Wilson would have been willing to liquidate anything by now. He went to see Major Duffy eagerly.

For Waddell to have won over Duffy was a master stroke. He was a bristling little Irishman, who had started as a bandsman in the Guards and become drum major. It was said that in his day he had been the only drum major to throw his stick over the archway of Wellington barracks as the battalion marched in and to catch it on the other side. He had been in the van of the old colonel's "bull brigade".

No one knew how he got his commission, or when, or where. But he had been with the regiment in peace time. He hugged its traditions, he knew all its jokes, and would have died rather than acknowledge the lifeless title which the War Office insensibly tried to impose on it—"141st Regiment, R.A.C."

For weeks it had seemed to Wilson that Duffy was fighting an inner battle of his own, trying to decide if he should support the interloper. What had made up his mind? Perhaps he had seen the unpleasant truth, that only Waddell could hammer the regiment into anything worthy of its name.

"Well," he said, "you know how often we have an ENSA?"

"Once a month."

"And a dance?"

"I don't remember any dance," said Wilson.

"Right," said Duffy. "From now on there's going to be something every night."

One by one the recalcitrant relics of the "Old Guard" disappeared—to staff jobs, training regiments, ostensible promotions in regiments far away. Fatigues were cut down to almost nothing. Training came forward. The tanks went out every day. Troop runs gave way to squadron runs, and squadron runs to manoeuvres with the whole regiment.

Wilson went on another course. He stayed in a mansion near Dorking and learned about mines—teller mines which blew the tracks off a tank; mines made of wood which produced no reaction on the electronic detector; "S" mines which sprang out of the ground and killed everyone round them with a hail of small steel balls.

"Every tank man must become his own Sapper," said the instructors, and when Wilson came back he had to run mines courses for the regiment.

Then, at the beginning of December, the regiment took its tanks into Ashford and loaded them on war-flats in the railway siding. It was a bitterly cold night. There was an air-raid warning, and searchlights probed the sky. For a moment it was possible to believe they were off to the real thing.

Twelve hours later they unloaded the tanks in Lewes. As each troop was ready, it motored off high on the South Downs.

For the next three days they marched and assembled, attacked, defended and counter-attacked, in a mock operation against the other two regiments of the brigade. At night the tanks were drawn up in a "laager"—a square with the guns of the guard tanks pointing outward. The C.O. would order a rum issue, and the crews would creep into their rain-lashed bivouacs.

One night, as they lay on a corner of the laager, Wilson's troop was attacked by a raiding group of the enemy's infantry. They came in throwing thunder-flashes, yelling and waving their rifles. In the old days the men would have let themselves be captured, for the enemy was supposed to be having better rations and living off field-kitchens. But now, by some common impulse, they started to use their knees and fists.

When the yells and swearing subsided, the enemy withdrew into the darkness, followed by a solitary jeer. In the morning there were four enemy rifles to be handed in to the quartermaster.

On the last day of the exercise the umpires made the regiment take up a hopeless position in a big depression. On every side they could see the enemy, hull-down, waiting to close in.

Waddell called an order group. The word went round that the umpires were not to be "in" on it. When the squadron commanders came back and passed on their orders, the crews became tense and conspiratorial. They backed out the vehicles from their defence positions and formed them up in a close square, facing one way. The commanders sat waiting for the word across the wireless.

"Hello all stations Zebra One—advance!"

In a solid mass the regiment debouched. For a second or two it was slow going, then the ground sloped downwards.

26

Going downhill with the engine governor sabotaged, a Churchill IV could do twenty-five miles per hour. Suddenly everyone was doing twenty-five—including the C.O. A few intrepid drivers took their tanks out of gear and went rolling ahead at speeds undreamed of by the designers.

It was mad and untactical and intoxicating.

Ahead of Wilson, two forty-ton tanks went crashing into each other, throwing off a catherine-wheel of sparks. Then they broke their clinch and raced on separately, leaving a litter of torn-off track guards.

Suddenly they were through the main line of the enemy. Some umpires waved red flags, but no one took notice. They swept past a copse. A platoon of anti-tank gunners stood open-mouthed by their half-concealed weapons; they hadn't seen anything like it before.

Half a mile further on the regiment pulled up on a hillside and troops and squadrons sorted themselves out. Not a single tank had broken down.

When they got back to Ashford, everybody was happy. They had put something over on the rest of the brigade, and the Brigade Commander had been pleased too.

Wilson became busy with entertainments. He filled four nights a week and sometimes five. But despite all efforts there was still about seven hundred pounds in the P.R.I. The C.O. was prodding him about Christmas arrangements. "It's got to be a real good show."

"Yes," said the fatherly Quartermaster-Captain, who'd just been given four hundred pounds to buy turkeys and beer. "It'd better be slap-up. For some poor benders it'll be the last."

Christmas was a great success. Food and beer were almost unlimited. The married men had their wives down. In the evening they all went into the new NAAFI, where the

27

stoves were at last red hot with a superior quality of coal, and watched a show of the regiment's own making.

Two inseparable madmen, who were always in and out of detention together, did an apache dance in tights.

Westwell, the Wireless Officer and a professional actor, gave the Crispin's Day speech from *Henry V*—an impressive performance, marred only by the reappearance of one of the madmen, naked but for a red and yellow "Damaged and Coming Out of Action" flag tied tightly across his behind.

William Douglas Home gave a perfect impersonation of the C.O. The cheers were thunderous, but there was no malice in them. As far as the men were concerned, Waddell had arrived.

II

TOP SECRET

"HELLO, Benzy, coming on the passion wagon to-night?"

Benzecry was a tall, spidery boy, a year or two older than Wilson. He belonged to "C" squadron, one of Duffy's officers.

"Sorry," he said. "I'm off on a course tomorrow."

"What kind of a course?"

"Oh, I don't know really. Some sort of course up in Suffolk."

"Too bad."

Wilson walked through the mess. It was empty except for a few majors and captains reading newspapers. Then he saw MacFarland.

"Hello, Mac, coming on the passion wagon?"

"Sorry, I'm off on a course."

"What, you too? "

"Yes."

"What's it on?"

"I don't know."

Damn them. What was all the mystery? He went on and found the Doctor.

Everyone liked the Doctor, with his long lean face and eyes which blinked surprisedly behind their horn-rimmed glasses whenever people laughed at his jokes.

When the regiment had got orders to paint names on the

tanks, each beginning with the letter "S", he had suggested "Syphilis" for his ambulance half-track. But the C.O. turned it down.

They went into Ashford to the Saracen's Head. But even the doctor's inexhaustible anecdotes couldn't dispel the after-Christmas gloom and Wilson's uncomfortable feeling that things were happening which he didn't know about.

At the end of January, Wilson lost his troop. Ever since he went on the mines course, his Squadron Commander had complained that he was never with the tanks. Now he was asking for a replacement. Wilson felt sick with anger. To lose one's troop now was like being sentenced to extinction.

"Look," said William Home, who as temporary Adjutant had intercepted the Squadron Commander's letter, "if you feel like that about it, go in and see the C.O. now. Ask to go to another squadron. I'll hold up the letter till this afternoon."

But Wilson shook his head. Incoherent with bitterness, he was looking out of the orderly room window, trying to hold back the tears which even now, at twenty years of age, would constantly trap him when he most needed to express himself.

A few minutes later the letter went in, and Waddell sent for him.

"I see your point of view," he said. "But the Squadron Commander says ye've neglected the troop, and I'm not going against that."

That night in mess was a full-dinner night.

"What are all ye subalterns doing?" said Waddell. "Make a party."

Wilson would have liked to go out, to weep in the fields, to drink a bottle of whisky, to find a girl he'd met in the

Saracen's Head. But there was no escape. Dutifully, with the others, he helped to push back the leather arm-chairs and the billiard table, and one of the Scots officers whom Waddell had lately imported began to dance a reel.

After some singing and some more dancing, Waddell himself joined in. Presently the whole mess was going round in a wild Scottish dance in which everyone joined hands. Then suddenly with a shout and a whoop everyone let go and went reeling back towards the walls.

Wilson staggered back, three or four others with him, till they fell across a couch and tipped it over.

As they were sorting themselves out he looked sideways and there on the carpet was Waddell's flushed face, a foot from his own. Suddenly he felt that if only that face would smile, Waddell would give him another job and everything would be all right.

But Waddell did not smile. His eyes were as cold as ever. In that moment Wilson saw that for his C.O. this was no party, but an exercise in raising officers' morale. And he knew that Waddell could have no interest in re-instating him, because now he had become a piece of grit in the regimental machinery.

In the end Wilson went to the Reserve Squadron. It wasn't a proper squadron. One didn't have a troop there. When the regiment went to war, Reserve was to send up men and vehicles to replace casualties. Meanwhile they trained newcomers and absorbed throw-outs.

One of the other throw-outs was Harry Barrow. Wilson had no clear idea how Harry got there. But he remembered him on a scheme, and the Squadron Commander telling him to take his tanks across a certain piece of ground. After acknowledging the message Harry had forgotten to switch back to intercom, so that his orders to his driver were

31

broadcast round the regiment: "Frig 'em, Bob, let's go our
own way."

The commander of Reserve was William Home. William
seemed resigned to it. He had been off on leave to fight
a parliamentary by-election, in which he attacked Mr.
Churchill and the policy of unconditional surrender. He had
lost. The electors, like the regiment, refused to take him
seriously.

"I say, sir, the new tanks are in."

The little lance-corporal in Reserve squadron office was
almost breathless. It was refreshing to see someone excited
in Reserve.

Wilson and Barrow walked down to the tank park, and
there were the Mark VIIs. The Technical staff had been
unloading them during the night.

"They look a bit heavy," said Barrow.

They climbed aboard and looked one over.

As with most tanks, the turret was filled with the mechanism of the two guns—the main gun and the Besa machine-
gun. Behind the guns, in the back of the turret, were
the two wireless sets: the "A" set for talking across the
squadron network, the "B" set for talking with tanks in the
same troop. The wireless operator/gun-loader had just room
to stand on the right of the gun; the gunner had a seat on the
left. The commander had a little platform at the gunner's
back. The driver and co-driver sat forward in the front of
the hull.

But the Mark VII's equipment was a great advance
on that of the earlier Churchills. Instead of a six-pounder,
the main gun was a seventy-five millimetre. There were new
wheels for elevating it and traversing the turret, and a
system of wires and electric switches for firing. Forward,

there was a big ball-mounting for the co-driver's machine-gun. And the front and sides of the hull had been thickened with enormous steel plates. When you opened the driver's visor you saw the full depth of the armour—seven inches.

Duffy's squadron took over their Mark VIIs first. Then "A" and "B" squadrons. Finally Reserve got theirs. They ticked off the items on the tool list, and swabbed the grease off the guns, and drew paint from the stores to stencil on the divisional signs. But just as the paint was drying, word came round to paint the signs out. The regiment wasn't in the Division any more; it wasn't even in the Brigade.

"Christ Almighty," said Barrow, "doesn't anybody tell us what's going on?"

By the end of February another bunch of subalterns had come back tight-lipped from the course in Suffolk. All were from "C" squadron. It was humiliating enough that others should be chosen for a job and not oneself; but far more humiliating that they wouldn't even discuss it.

Wilson did everything possible to find out. That is to say, he ceased to ask questions and merely listened. But all he heard was the name of the regiment which ran the courses in Suffolk—the 43rd R.T.R.—and the phrase "experimental unit".

Barrow was irritated too. They were naming a trio of new tanks—the last to be delivered.

"What shall it be?"

"How about 'Stalingrad', 'Stalin' and 'Samovar'?" said Wilson.

"Lovely," said Barrow. "That'll shake 'em."

For good measure they painted a big red hammer and sickle on Stalingrad's backside. But unfortunately everybody in authority was too busy to notice it.

33

A few days later the regiment went up to Westmorland to fire the new guns. When they came back from the ranges there was a strange sergeant at Ashford. He stood at the entrance to the tank park, watching them drive in. Later he was seen wandering over the area where they did their training. He had a little van, which he parked near the orderly room.

"Who is he?" said Wilson.

"I don't know, but I'll find out," said Barrow.

He came back.

"Field Security Police."

Tactical training continued as before.

One day Wilson took some crews to a distant part of the area to get them away from the ground they knew by heart. It was a cold February day, momentarily lit by sunshine. They came over a rise and there, in front of them, was a company of Pioneers. They were building something.

He took the tanks closer. There were dumps of scaffolding and corrugated-iron sheets and, a little further on, the foundations of some concrete structures against an earth bank.

"New hangars," said someone in the crews.

"Piss-houses," said someone else.

Beyond these simple necessities imagination ended.

Back in the mess, no one knew anything either. But it was only the officers back from Suffolk who positively recoiled from knowing.

Wilson and Barrow were discussing all the secrecy again.

"It can't be the Mark VIIs. There's frig all to them," said Barrow. "Anyway, half the bloody railwaymen in England have seen them by now."

No. It wasn't the Mark VIIs—at least not by themselves.

34

But that night Wilson broke in on the secret. He was orderly officer, one of whose more irksome duties was to turn out the guard. So that the guard would be surprised, he would report to the Adjutant and draw from his cap a slip of paper marked "midnight–2", "2–4", "4–6" or "6–8".

Within the hours on his slip of paper the Orderly Officer would make his rounds, the Sergeant of the Guard would record the turn-out on his report, and the Orderly Officer would certify that the guard was alert and supplied with a can of hot cocoa. ·

Wilson had gone to draw his slip, but just as the Adjutant was holding out his cap he was called away by the buzzer from the C.O.'s room. In his absence it was impossible not to see a typewritten sheet of paper, with a notebook thrown hastily across it. It was headed "43rd R.T.R.—Courses". Then the notebook intervened. Just visible at the bottom was the fascinating, cryptic end of a sentence ". . . Flails, AVREs, Congas, Crocodiles and other devices."

"Sorry to keep you waiting," said the Adjutant. "What did you draw?"

"Midnight to two."

"I hope you didn't cheat."

In the corner of the ante-room the "C" squadron course boys were gathered round tankards of beer. The opportunity was too good to miss.

Wilson made his choice. AVRE looked fascinating, but he didn't know how to pronounce it. A Flail, he knew, was a tank with lashing chains which blew up mines. Crocodile sounded dramatic—like a vast machine weighing thousands of tons which advanced with steel jaws to scoop up battalions of infantry.

He ordered a beer and advanced on the little circle.

"Can someone please tell me, just what the hell is a Crocodile?"

Everyone stopped talking and put down their beer mugs. MacFarland began looking attentively at the ornamentation of the pseudo-gothic fireplace. Benzecry was blushing ridiculously. He was intensely upright and honest. Even in the service of his country he couldn't carry deception very far.

"You'd better sign the Official Secrets Act," he said.

Everybody signed the Secrets Act in the end. It was like the touch of a wand. Suddenly you could be told everything.

The Crocodile equipment hadn't arrived yet. But they were expecting it every day. "It's terrific," said Benzecry. "No one else has anything like it—even the Yanks." Meanwhile the "C" squadron boys were getting ready a disused farmhouse, away on the far side of the training area, where they were going to give instruction.

A large stretch of the training area had been discreetly wired in, with the wire hidden behind bushes. The guards had been reorganised. The Field Security sergeant had taken up quarters in the village. From there he ranged about the countryside. He wore civilian clothes now. Once Wilson saw him in the Saracen's Head, listening in the background while a captain was talking to a girl.

The equipment came, as the Mark VIIs had done, by night. The first Wilson saw of it was when he walked out to the squadron office one morning. There in the hard clear light on the training area stood a curious object with two enormous rubber tyres. It was shaped like the blunt prow of a boat, and in place of the bowsprit was a big steel pipe cased in armour plating. He went closer and saw that the pipe was meant to be coupled to the back of a tank.

Just then Benzecry passed, on his way to the farmhouse. "Have a good look," he said. "You'll start training to-morrow."

"Why have you parked the thing here?" said Wilson.

"Because it mustn't go in the tank park. And if anyone shows a trailer within five miles of a Mark VII, except inside the training area, he'll be"— Benzecry looked for the phrase —"shot in the Tower," he said.

They went to the farmhouse with notebooks which were to be filled with diagrams and put under lock and key each evening. Each instructor had his own lecture room, and the big charts showing wiring circuits and pressure systems made a splash of bright colour on the crumbling walls.

Sometimes Wilson would turn away from the charts and look through the latticed window across the training area. Away out of sight the first of the Crocodiles was being tested, and every now and then a thick black cloud of smoke would rise above the trees and drift off raggedly in the wind.

"Stand back, they're going to pressure up."

The lectures were finished. The theory had been memorised. The notebooks had been burnt. They were standing round the whole apparatus—tank and trailer linked up—while a demonstration crew manipulated a system of valves and gauges. There had been a change to the tank since Wilson last saw it; instead of the co-driver's machine-gun there was now an ugly little nozzle with two metal tongues above it like the points of a sparking-plug.

While they stood there, there was continuous hissing and ticking from the trailer—the sort of noise a locomotive makes as it waits to take out its train. Then the noise ceased. The crew shut the trailer door and climbed into the tank.

"First they'll do a run to show you everything," said Benzecry. "Trenches, dug-outs, pill-boxes, houses—the whole lot." The spectators climbed on to a bank. They were looking at what the pioneers had built: a section of mock battlefield. The Crocodile lay below them, an impatient dragon licking its lips.

There was a little burst of fire, like a struck match, above the nozzle. ("Testing the spark," said Benzecry.) The tank began to move forward.

It went towards the first target, a concrete pill-box. Suddenly there was a rushing in the air, a vicious hiss. From the front of the tank a burning yellow rod shot out. Out and out it went, up and up, with a noise like the slapping of a thick leather strap. The rod curved and started to drop, throwing off burning particles. It struck the concrete with a violent smack. A dozen yellow fingers leapt out from the point of impact, searching for cracks and apertures. All at once the pill-box was engulfed in fire—belching, twisting, red-roaring fire. And clouds of queer-smelling, grey-black smoke.

"A bit high," shouted Benzecry.

As he spoke there was another rushing. This time the rod went clean through an embrasure, smacking, belching, roaring. The flame shot out through the back of the pill-box, fanning like a blow-torch.

"Lovely, lovely!"

The Crocodile was on the trenches now; the trenches were zig-zag and the flame went chasing round the corners. It was quite a technique. You could count the number of bounces it made, like skimming stones on the sea.

Then it advanced on the houses. They were made of corrugated iron wired to steel scaffolding. Their fronts were square with a door and four windows; the kind of house that children draw.

The flame poured out for ten or fifteen seconds, drumming on the iron like thunder. The sheets began to buckle.

38

One of them blew away. The flame-gunner changed aim, and the rod poured in through an upper storey.

"Now they'll do a wet shot," said Benzecry.

The Crocodile moved to another house. There was the same hiss and slapping, but the rod was not ignited. The stream of colourless liquid poured into the house till everything was saturated. Then there was a shot of flame. Fire raced all along the structure. Beyond the door, where the liquid had collected in a pool, it rose in a fierce red cyclone. It leapt and roared towards a smoke cloud which already hid the sun. The heat blew back on the spectators.

At last the fire died down, though flames still flickered from a hundred tiny patches of half-burnt fuel. Benzecry led them forward. Beneath the creaking metal, the ground was black and smoking. Wherever the flame had touched, there was a silvery film, like a snail's trail.

"All right," said Benzecry, "let's have lunch."

Wilson was trying to extinguish a spot of the liquid which had got on to his boot. It clung and burned, however hard he tried to shake it off. In the end he wiped it off, still burning, on some grass.

For the next eight weeks they worked hard on the Crocodiles. The makers were sending down the trailers as fast as they finished them. Each one came up with a pile of wooden cases containing the "conversion kit" for the tank—the heavy towing link, the armoured fuel pipe which ran to the flame gun, the electrical equipment and air lines. It was like Meccano.

Every day the crews practised on the targets. They lunched off haversack rations. Their skins grew brown in the sun and their muscles hardened like steel with the lifting of the great drums of fuel. In the evening they went over the area putting matches to any drops that remained unburnt,

39

because the fuel was very secret. Then they walked home, too tired to talk, in the darkness.

They didn't see so much of Waddell now, he was always off to conferences. Then one morning everyone was excluded from the training area, except "C" squadron.

"What was it all about?" Wilson asked afterwards.

"A demonstration for V.I.P.s," said Benzecry.

"What V.I.P.s?"

"Oh, Americans and some British."

"Any one amusing?"

"One quite nice chap."

A few days after the King's visit "C" squadron went away. It happened very quietly. One day they had been there, and the next there were just their Nissen huts, spotless and empty with the bare beds and swept concrete floors. Wilson was sorry. They were by far the best squadron, and he wished he'd been going with them.

One night soon afterwards he was Orderly Officer again. As he sat in the duty room, the telephone rang. It was Duffy. His voice was faint and he sounded far away.

"Is the C.O. there?"

"Sorry, sir. He's not in the mess."

"Who's speaking?"

"Wilson."

"All right, Wilson. Give him a message. Make sure you get it exactly——"

Duffy paused, and Wilson could feel him working out the sentences.

"Tell him I've just met my mother-in-law. She seems very fond of the babies, and she thinks they should stop indoors from now on. A couple are going on ahead and she's given them a room to themselves. Oh, yes. And tell him we're all getting something good for our eyesight."

Beyond the open window the night was still, and the world was very empty.

A week or two later both "A" and "B" squadrons went away, and Reserve was left to pack up the spare tanks and take them to a place which turned out to be Farnborough. Whatever was happening, Farnborough was going to be in the very back of it. In the excitement of the past months, Wilson had almost forgotten that he had no troop; now that he remembered, he felt sadder and angrier than ever. Once again he was assailed by the fear that the war would be over before he got into it.

The arrangements for the move were that the tanks went off on transporter lorries and Wilson stayed behind to take up the trailers in batches of three.

"Choose a different route each time," said William Home.

The towing trucks arrived—gargantuan Scammells with a lusty, throaty roar. He took the first batch through Guildford and the second through Croydon. When he came to the last he took it through London, across Blackfriars Bridge, up the Strand and down Whitehall.

"Let her full out," he told the driver as they roared and rattled by the War Office, and he hoped it shook the foundations.

III

EMBARKATION GROUP

THERE were so many troops and tanks in Farnborough that although one knew they could only be support waves, it seemed that the whole army was there. The squadron was parked on a stretch of heath adjoining their barracks. It was an ancient barracks, with a mess full of other regiments' silver, and the permanent staff—officers and orderlies—trying to act as if nothing were happening.

The crews were waterproofing when Wilson arrived—sealing up hatches and air vents for the wade from the landing ships, and fitting the charges which would blow off the sealing as they reached dry land. It was good to see that at least they weren't landing in some port, like tourists. But there was no secrecy about it. Civilians stood watching from the road, and if there wasn't an officer about, girls would come over and chat with the men as they plugged in the black adhesive.

At six o'clock each evening everyone stopped work. After supper they walked through the long, blank barrack-roads to Aldershot, where Canadian privates fought outside pubs and the nyloned legs of Canadian WAACs were pursued by British wolf-calls.

There was a curious uneasiness in Aldershot and Farnborough in the first, warm days of June. No one knew where he was going or even if he'd get there. The Canadians had been waiting for action for nearly four years. They were so used to it that now they couldn't stop drinking till somebody dragged them away. For the British it was different. They were all keyed up. Everything was impending for them; and everything was withheld, like those slender nyloned legs which tapped down the Aldershot pavements.

Then one evening there was a sound of aircraft. They were friendly aircraft, going south. The sound went on through the night. Once Wilson went out and looked up, and up against the stars he saw the long bodies of gliders.

Early next morning William came into the room.

"Get up," he said. "The invasion's started."

"I know," said Wilson. "But where?"

"Normandy."

Normandy. He tried to picture the French coast, but it was too vague. In connection with the invasion he'd always thought of places that seemed doomed by history— Calais, Dunkirk, Flanders, Picardy, Zeebrugge. But Normandy wasn't among them. It had no business with war.

A day or two after D-Day, when waterproofing was finished, Wilson and three other subalterns were ordered to go down to an embarkation group which was assembling at Eastbourne. They took a train which would give them a night in London. Then Wilson remembered that it was two days from his twenty-first birthday and that, before letters stopped, his parents had talked about celebrating it. There was one more train into Kent. It stopped about fifteen miles short of his home, but he took it.

Once or twice as he walked through the wet night a car overtook him, refusing to stop. The road seemed endless, till he reached a wayside kiosk he knew, and telephoned the house. Then he went on into the silent town and up the hill where the house stood. Beyond a chink in the curtains a light was burning. It was ten to four.

"We thought you were already over the Channel," said his mother. She was crying a little. There was a cake on the table, and his father opened a bottle of whisky, holding it between his knees and prising off the cap with his one, strong hand.

"Many happy returns," he said. "God bless you."

They took their drinks and tried to find things to say. But in reality there was nothing. For the future—even the immediate future—was unknown, and the ordinary topics of conversation had no meaning any more. At last the effort of trying not to waste these last few hours together defeated itself. Wilson fell asleep in his chair.

When he woke up, his mother was calling him to catch the eight o'clock train. There was breakfast on the table, and coffee too hot to drink. Desperately he tried to think of something to tell her which would stop her worrying about him. But now it was too late. He kissed her good-bye and went out to the waiting taxi.

Beside the door, where the firewatcher's helmet hung, his father was waiting with his hand out.

"Good luck," he said.

The embarkation group at Eastbourne consisted of fifty tanks and lorries, due to be drawn into the machinery which would put them on the sea. There were three Crocodiles under an officer from the regiment, called Ward. They were being fitted with the mysterious "aid to eyesight" which Duffy had talked about on the telephone: a cupola with an all-round vision periscope, which the commander could rotate above his head.

There was nothing to do but wait. One of Wilson's companions was a lean, athletic Scot, with a fatal charm for women. The day after they arrived he found a girl-friend and moved out of his billet for the freer atmosphere of a hotel. The other was a gentle Roman Catholic, called Ian Sutherland Sherrif. He, too, was tempted to recklessness; but conscience held him back.

They spent their days in different bars and tea-shops, and at night they arranged to call the Scotsman in case there was an order to move.

For a week the war and the Invasion seemed to have passed them by. Then one evening as they came back to their billet, an anti-aircraft gun started firing. Another took it up, and quickly they were firing from all round the town.

"What are they after?" said Sherrif. "There isn't even a searchlight."

They looked out to sea, where the streams of tracer converged. Presently, from out of the snow-storm, six red dots appeared. They passed across the sky with a curious knocking sound, and when they were gone there were another six.

The guns fired often during the night. Next day everyone learned about flying-bombs, and the serial was put at six hours' notice to move.

When you reached the transit camp you knew you were at the end of the conveyor belt. They issued you with forty-eight hours' rations and a big box of maps, and reminded you to fill out the will form in your officer's book. Looking at the will form, Wilson wondered just what he had to leave. In his room at home was a desk he'd once bought. On it were his books—*The Poems of Catullus*, Bury's *History of Greece*, *Pilgrim's Progress*, the *Romance of Modern Invention*, and *Mounted Reconnaissance* 1912. Then there were his bicycle and fishing-rods. But who would want them? He went to sleep still wondering about it.

Next afternoon, when everything was ready, he attended to a few last details, like getting his boots repaired and going to the baker to buy a couple of loaves, for there would only be biscuits on the "other side". Then he went to the camp cinema. All through the film a sergeant kept coming into the hut to call the numbers of different serials, and men would get up with a grumble, casting their shadows on the screen. At last the film ended and he walked out into the daylight.

In a draughty marquee, there was tea in enamel mugs and thick uneatable slices of bread and jam. Sherrif was there, and the Scotsman, dressed in overalls for the journey. They swallowed some tea and picked up their kit and walked out to the road, where the drivers were warming up the tanks.

"What was the flick like?" said Sherrif.

"Well . . ." said Wilson, but couldn't remember.

The tanks clattered into Southampton. The trailers were fixed now; there was no more secrecy. People came out of their houses and stood watching them. Many of them waved and sometimes an old soldier with envious eyes would shout "Good luck, boys." Once they stopped and girls came and threw their arms round the drivers.

They moved on. The people were still watching; you couldn't see them any longer, but you sensed them. Then it started to rain, and there was only the dim red tail-lamp of the vehicle ahead in the drizzle. Stops became more frequent. Noisy despatch riders went fussing along the column, and presently there was the dark, portending odour of docks.

"Get on to the pavement and don't show lights."

They switched off engines. Somewhere in the silence, water gushed from a broken drain-pipe. It was a mean street. Nobody lived there. The houses had all been bombed.

And yet it had a kind of sanctity. Backwards, it led to London, or Birmingham, or Glasgow, or whatever was your home: turn back and walk, and sooner or later you'd get there. Forwards, it led to a loading-ramp—and beyond that? You just didn't know.

"Serial 56?"

Beneath a blue lamp the Embarkation Officer was ticking off the vehicles on a list. Ahead was the landing-ship— an enormous tunnel of light heaving gently on the water. The driver let in the clutch. The tank slewed round on the concrete and backed up the steel flap.

When Wilson woke, there was a steel bulkhead by his side; beneath him a hard mattress and the hum of the ship's engines. He threw off the blanket and went out on deck. There were three other landing-ships and a single destroyer nosing anxiously around them. Far to the west was another small group. Otherwise the sea was empty.

Ward came up and joined him.

"What about breakfast," he said.

They went down the swaying companionway and found a seaman. It was an American ship.

"Where do we eat?" said Wilson.

"Is you officers or enlisted men?"

"Officers."

"First door left, bud."

A couple of ship's officers were eating at the far end of the long table. They looked up and nodded and went on talking. A phlegmatic steward brought glasses of tomato juice.

"You like crispy bacon?"

"Yes," they said; and a few moments later he came back with a big plate crammed with bacon and eggs and rounds of fried pineapple.

47

After breakfast they put on their overalls and went down to the tank hold. It was like an enormous garage with a gallery running round and an electric lift at one end to hoist up vehicles to the deck above. The tanks were chained down to stop them slipping with the movement of the ship. She was heeling quite steeply now, and there was a reek of petrol.

"Well," said Ward, "we'd better take the plunge. Got your sick bags?"

Wilson patted the issue paper bags which he'd stuffed in his leg pocket and they summoned the crews.

The last job of waterproofing was done at sea. It meant fitting tall steel boxes to the engine air-intakes. On land it would have taken half an hour, but now, with the motion of the ship and the sickening petrol fumes, it seemed endless.

Once, when they'd got a box in place and were fixing the struts to hold it, a co-driver reached for his sick-bag and let everything fall with a clatter. Then one of the tanks broke loose. It was Ward's. With every heave of the ship it slid across the deck and crashed into the next vehicle. The noise brought a chief petty officer.

"Christ," he shouted. "Get hold of that goddam thing, or it'll go through the side of the ship!"

They fixed a new chain to the tank and waited for it to swing inwards. Then Ward ran in and fixed the chain to a deck shackle, before the tank swung out again. Each time the tank moved Ward ran in and tightened the chain a little further, standing between the sliding tank and the side of the ship.

When it was done he leaned against the tank, white and perspiring, clutching his paper bag.

Towards evening the waterproofing was finished and they

48

came out on deck. The sea had subsided and there was just a gentle swell. The other ships in the convoy had closed in and a number of others were visible.

"Listen," said Ward. "Do you hear the guns?"

Wilson strained to hear, but nothing came. They went below and lay on their bunks.

"Come on," said Ward.

The engines had stopped. The ship was strangely silent, as if nobody was aboard her any more. Wilson looked at his watch. It was seven o'clock.

They climbed the companion-way, and there was the coast.

It was startlingly close: a low line of sand, topped here and there with green. Inland were woods, and beyond them a long smudge of smoke. Now he could hear the guns, drumming and throbbing incessantly in the still air.

For a moment neither of them spoke.

All around stood the invasion fleet—landing-ships and merchantmen, and in the distance, against the setting sun, the long, sombre shapes of the warships. One of them blinked with its signal lamp, and the message was answered by a lamp on the shore. Over on the left there was a village. The spire of a church glinted red and gold.

"What is it?" said Wilson.

"Courseulles," someone answered. And while they watched, the sun left the church and lit the underside of a cloud.

The water was alive with launches and amphibious trucks; they skimmed to and fro like summer-evening insects on a pool, taking off stores from the merchantmen. Presently a small boat came up to the landing-ship. An army captain with an armband came aboard.

49

"You're going in now," he said. "Drive straight ahead and you'll steer clear of underwater craters."

In the hold, the ship's crew turned on the big ventilator fans, which made it safe to start the tank engines. The tank crews unshackled the tanks and began to warm them up. Then the great bow-doors opened, and a steel flap was let down into the water.

Wilson drove down the flap, and next moment all that showed above water was his waddling turret and the uncouth ironmongery attached to the air intakes. There was the curious sensation of breasting through the sea while the tank tracks below ran firmly on the sea bed.

They passed the wreck of a landing craft. He hoped they were going straight. The underwater craters from the D-Day bombardment were enormous. In some of the earlier serials tanks had disappeared in them and were never seen again.

"I hope we're not heading for frigging England," called the driver over the intercom. He was two feet below the water and steering blind.

When they reached the beach there was a route marked with white tapes. The tanks swung over the sand and pulled up in the place where they were supposed to assemble.

"Where the hell are the rest?" said a Beach Officer irritably. It was almost dark, and he kept looking across the dunes to where a steel-helmeted crew stood by their Bofors anti-aircraft gun.

The other tanks came lolloping up, their crews grinning.

"All right. Follow the motor-cycle and get out of here," shouted the Beach Officer.

They moved off—and a second later the guns started firing. It began far away with the kettle-drum roll of an Oerlikon. Then the sound started from another direction, and another, and another. Suddenly there was a roar of propellers and a pale pair of wings flashed overhead. In a moment the dunes seemed to split in a sheet of flame. The earth shook with the crack of bombs.

When the tanks were clear, Wilson took his eyes from the tail-lamp of the motor-cycle and looked back. The whole fleet had joined in. Lines of red tracer were rising and falling, sweeping and converging, down the length of the narrow beach-head.

They spent the night in a field, mid-way between the guns on the beach and the guns on the front. When they woke up the sun was shining. On the slope beyond, a battery of big five-fives lay momentarily silent beneath their sagging camouflage nets.

"Madame, est-ce que vous avez du lait?"

The old woman put down her churns and took the queer money with a sigh. Wilson went back with the milk, and they lay in the sun, waiting for someone to tell them where to go.

In the afternoon a guide arrived to lead them to the regiment. All the roads were thick with chalky, white dust, and in every field there were infantry or guns or lorries.

"Strewth," said the operator, who stood beside Wilson in the rattling turret, "if Jerry drops a bomb, he can't miss."

But he laughed as he spoke. Everyone was in curiously high spirits. Once they stopped for the two-hourly halt to let the engines cool and a party of R.A.S.C. drivers ran over to the tank crews with a bucket of hot, sweet tea they'd been brewing for themselves. It was something, you felt, that could happen just once in a war.

When they'd finished, the crews slapped the Service

Corps drivers on the back. They moved off again, joking and laughing, towards the dark woods where the guns grumbled. Then at a bend in the road they pulled in to let a column of tank-transporters pass, carrying Churchills.

As the transporters came near, you could see there was something wrong with the Churchills. Several had their turrets and guns askew. Closer, and you could see the holes where the shots had gone in. Wilson counted the tanks . . . eleven, twelve, thirteen. They belonged to a regiment that had been in the same brigade at Ashford. After that no one spoke much.

They reached the regiment in the evening. A thunderstorm was coming up and you couldn't tell the gun flashes from the lightning. Harry Barrow stood by the roadside to guide them into harbour, his hands on his hips, every gesture proclaiming that he'd been there three days before you. As soon as they were in everyone ran over to him.

"How's it going, Harry? Has the regiment been in? Are 'C' squadron with you? How's Benzecry, MacFarland, Duffy . . ."

He held up his hand and grinned.

"The regiment's doing fine," he said, "fighting seven Panzer divisions. Mac, you're going out to 'A' tonight, and Ian's going to 'C'. They want you quick." Then he paused and told them who'd been killed.

You had known there were going to be casualties. But now it was suddenly hard to realise that all those men were dead. You saw them again in some action or posture long forgotten; and oddly it wasn't the ones to whom you were most attached whose memory disturbed you.

Sherrif and the Scotsman came back from their tanks, lugging their kit.

"Goodbye, Ian; goodbye, Mac. Look after yourselves."

52

They disappeared in a jeep towards their new squadrons, and Wilson walked back to the crews, who were refuelling. He was thinking of a lieutenant in "B" squadron with a small, twisted mouth, who once in an argument had spat out the word "shit". It was impossible to believe that that mouth was silenced for ever.

IV

CROCODILES, TIGERS, PANTHERS

NEXT morning, when Wilson and Ward had reported to the Adjutant, Barrow told them the truth about the Crocodiles; the flame thrower was terrific, but the tank itself a death trap. There followed a little catechism about British and German tanks.

"What do the Germans have most of?"

"Panthers. The Panther can slice through a Churchill like butter from a mile away."

"And how does a Churchill get a Panther?"

"It creeps up on it. When it reaches close quarters, the gunner tries to bounce a shot off the underside of the Panther's gun mantlet. If he's lucky, it goes through a piece of thin armour above the driver's head."

"Has anybody ever done it?"

"Yes. Davis in 'C' squadron. He's back with head-quarters now, trying to recover his nerve."

"What's next on the list?"

"Tigers. The Tiger can get you from a mile and a half."

"And how does a Churchill get a Tiger?"

"It's supposed to get within two hundred yards and put a shot through the periscope."

"Has anyone ever done it?"

"No."

Barrow told them about a lot of other things—about the self-propelled high-velocity guns in German Mark IV tank chassis, which lay waiting for the British in every little copse, and about the eighty-eights, which the German anti-tank gunners concealed behind hedges till you were almost on top of them. Then there were the Panzerfausts—vicious little rockets fired by the enemy infantry; when they struck a tank they punched a hole no thicker than a pencil through the armour, and poured in fire and steel fragments more deadly than any shell.

But there was one consolation for Churchill crews. When the Churchill was hit it caught fire three times out of five, and it could take up to ten seconds for the fire to sweep through from the engine compartment to the turret. The American Sherman caught fire every time, and the flames swept through in about three seconds. Many British regiments had Shermans, and the Germans called them "tommy cookers".

"Well," said Harry when he'd finished, "it's no use fretting. They'll want you soon enough. Let's go into Bayoo."

Bayoo was a little town in north-west Calvados, famous for an ancient tapestry, which, as far as the British army was concerned, had entered an era of peace and plenty about D-Day-plus-one. When Wilson and Barrow got there, it already had every sign of civilisation; that is to say, the shops were full of fountain pens and silk stockings, officers and soldiers from base units were sitting in cool bistros sipping vin blanc, and all the necessary establishments had been marked out of bounds.

"What the hell can one do?" said Barrow.

After wandering round for a while, he bought a bottle of Chanel No. 5 for Mrs. Barrow, and they motored sadly back to the regiment, where everyone was digging slit trenches against the nightly air raid.

It soon appeared that digging slit trenches was the main occupation at headquarters. There was really nothing else to do, for all the squadrons were out, attached to different formations.

Every evening the C.O. would come back in his scout car, covered in dust and talking about some "exercise" he'd watched. But apart from Waddell, almost the only two officers who went up those last mysterious miles to the front were the Technical Adjutant and the R.E.M.E. captain, Drysdale.

After a couple of days, Wilson started begging lifts with Drysdale on his nightly visits to one or other of the squadrons. They would set off at sunset. The squadrons were harboured off the road between Tilly and Caen, where the war had got stuck for the moment. As you approached the forward area, the ground became littered with battle debris— burned-out vehicles and dead cows, hugely inflated, spreading a nauseous smell. At nearly every cross-roads you came on a group of charred buildings with bullet-spattered Dubonnet and St. Raphael signs. Up on the Tilly road were ten or twelve Panthers, knocked out by rocket-firing aircraft. They looked enormous, with their long guns and thick, sloping armour; and they were said to do thirty miles an hour.

Drysdale pointed out the places where the regiment had been in action. One was a little village called La Senaudière, where the wreck of a Panther and the wreck of a Crocodile stood facing each other. It was the Panther that Davis had got with a shot off the gun mantlet. He had just come up to the cross-roads with his sergeant, when the Panther loomed out of the smoke. For a moment the Panther hesitated between its two targets, till its long gun swung slowly over and fired point blank into the sergeant's tank.

56

Then it moved back on Davis. His gunner fired when the muzzles of the two guns were almost touching. The whole action took about ten seconds.

One day they went up to do a demolition. A Crocodile had been knocked out and stood at a place which might be lost in a counter-attack. It was Benzecry's. Benzecry had always been grumbling about the old style of periscope, which never let the tank commander see properly. He must have been delighted to get the new cupola: it was a wonderful thing, with all-round vision, just like the German ones. But no one had amended the anti-tank gunners' identification chart. One misty morning Benzecry came out of action and was taken for a Panther.

Wilson went up to the tank which was lying in an orchard with an ugly charred hole in the driving compartment.

"I wouldn't look inside," said Drysdale.

They opened up the trailer, which for some reason hadn't caught fire, and packed slabs of guncotton against the flame-fuel tanks. When it was ready, they finished the job that the British M.10 had started.

Back at regimental headquarters they bore their inactivity manfully. There was a heated argument about the siting of the mess tent. The tent had arrived, along with an issue of wooden lavatory seats, about D-plus-20. William Home, the mess president, had pitched it in a little arbour, far from the view of prying Focke-Wulfs.

All would have been well but for the Sanitary Corporal, a wizened old soldier with the British Empire Medal, who believed that the efficiency of his services was important to morale. He had waited for the lavatory seats with anxiety, and now that they had come he had a place reserved for them.

As the mess sat down to its first organised dinner, the proximity of the corporal's choice was all too apparent. It had to be decided if the mess or the other establishment would be moved to an exposed site on the hillside.

In the end, consideration for the welfare of the men prevailed. As evening drew on and the noise of aircraft was heard, officers' dinners were taken a little more hurriedly, but in return there was a fine view across the surrounding country, with its still woods and ripening cornfields.

After a while the nightly air raids grew monotonous. But the digging of trenches continued. At first they had been slits in the ground beside the bivouacs. Now whole pits were dug, and the bivouacs let into them. Each day the pits would be enlarged a little and the bivouacs sunk deeper.

Everyone who could seemed to be getting out of headquarters. Harry Barrow had gone, and Ward had gone. The latest to go was Pooh Harvey. He'd never once taken out the four headquarters tanks, and now he'd got himself posted to "A" squadron.

One afternoon Wilson and some other officers were bathing in a lazy stream which flowed at the end of the field where the bivouacs were.

"Duffy's in camp," said one of the others casually.

Immediately Wilson jumped up and pulled on his clothes. He ran through the lines of tents, buttoning up his blouse as he went. And there at the top was Duffy, about to get into his scout car.

"Hello," said Duffy surprised.

"Do you have a minute to spare, sir?"

He looked at his watch. "One exactly. What is it?"

"I want to be posted to your squadron."

Panther in a Normandy farm.

Churchill Mark VII Crocodile and trailer.

"Pressuring up".

Loading a high-pressure nitrogen bottle.

Wilson saw some doubt running through Duffy's mind. He'd been used to picking his officers as he pleased, and it was at once clear that Duffy had never considered him.

"I don't have a spare troop at the moment."

"I know, sir. I thought perhaps I could go in a sergeant's place."

Duffy smiled slightly, as if flattered that people should want to go to his squadron so much.

"Well, I'll think about it."

He vanished in the scout car in a cloud of dust, and Wilson walked back dejectedly through the bivouac area, where the trenches were now so deep that you had to shout to reach the people in the bottom.

That night he went up with Drysdale to "A" squadron. They were lying at the east end of the Tilly road, among some woods. If anything, the battle debris was thickest there. At every other cross-roads was a burned-out British armoured car. The role of armoured cars was horribly final. They were sent ahead to explore some feature, and if they didn't come back you knew the enemy were holding it.

These armoured cars had met an advancing S.S. division. Then there had been a battle, and after many days the S.S. had been pushed back to a ridge a few miles inland. Drysdale swung the jeep off the road and into the clearing where the squadron harboured its transport. As they came in it was plain there was something wrong.

"What's up?" said Drysdale.

" It's Mr. Harvey," said a sergeant.

Two days before, Harvey had gone in with an attack and lost a track as he milled about on the objective. It was a simple repair. But as he did it a counter-attack came in and the rest of the squadron was forced to fall back. Now, that morning, the squadron had helped retake the place. They found Harvey's tank and the tools laid out on the ground around it. Harvey and his crew had been lined up against a farmhouse wall and shot.

Wilson thought of Harvey with his big, bear-like body and a trick he'd had at parties of being able to waggle his ears. The idea of him facing an S.S. firing squad was utterly incongruous. He wanted to shout aloud, to do something to deny that it was possible. But next moment he wondered with the selfish fear, which was never to be far away in battle: would they shoot all captured Crocodile crews from now on?

Two mornings later as he walked away from breakfast, he met the C.O.

"Oh, Wilson." (The last time Waddell had spoken to him was at the interview at Ashford.)

"Yes, sir."

"Major Duffy's asking for a subaltern. He's going on an exercise soon. You'd better go up right away."

Wilson went off to the transport lines to get a truck; and when Waddell was out of sight, he ran.

Later, you'd never dare tell anyone that you'd rushed to get into action. But it was true. To get into action was an imperative urge you never questioned. The war in the bridgehead had lasted four weeks. You couldn't foresee that it was going to last six more. When it collapsed you wanted to share the triumph and relief of those who'd been in it.

Thus he was supremely happy as he jolted in the truck towards the Tilly road. He was happy despite what had happened to Harvey and Benzecry and Davis and a dozen others in the regiment. He didn't want to kill. Killing was incidental. He just wanted to be at the front.

When he reached the squadron, Duffy was standing by his tent. Wilson wondered what place he was going to be given, but before he could ask, Duffy came up to him.

"You're taking MacFarland's troop," he said.

Wilson had no idea why Duffy had suddenly taken the troop from MacFarland, who had seen so much action. He unloaded his kit and went over to the troop where Mac-Farland was waiting to hand over. He looked weary and empty, and Wilson tried to hide his own high spirits.

In England there had been elaborate formalities when you took over a troop: an inspection on the tanks and guns; a check of all the tools and equipment; half a dozen papers to sign. Now there was nothing. He waited while Mac-Farland took out his kit from the troop leader's tank and carried it away to one of the supply trucks. Then he threw up his own on the engine deck.

The crews were getting their midday meal from the squadron cook-house. They had been told about the hand-over already, and when they came back in ones and twos with their mess-tins, they stood away at the end of the tank line, talking among themselves and occasionally throwing a mistrustful glance at their new commander, who had never been in action.

Presently the sergeant arrived. He was much older than Wilson. He had been in action since D-plus-three.

The sergeant lit a cigarette.

There was an awkward pause.

"I expect you'd like to meet the crews," he said.

He called them over and introduced them. There was the corporal, a not very friendly man, with a scrubby moustache; a tough-looking trooper who was to be Wilson's driver; and his co-driver/flame gunner, a young lance-corporal whom he found, to his relief, he had known at

Ashford. Finally the wireless operator and the seventy-five gunner, who were to take their places in the turret with him.

After that came the men of the sergeant's and corporal's crews. He tried to remember their names. According to the rules of what the army called "man-management" he ought to be asking them all about their background—what they were in civilian life; which of them were married; how many children they had. But looking at their faces, he knew that the only questions which mattered to them were the ones they would have liked to ask for themselves: whether he could read a map properly, and if he could tell a Panther from a Bren-gun carrier.

Two days later the squadron got orders to go up to the front. They drove out of harbour after tea. All the way up to the front Wilson had a quickened sense of small things round him—the smell of the road dust, the green, evening softness of the fields, the flutter of birds which flew off from the hedges as the tanks passed. As men from other units came out of their bivouacs to look at the Crocodiles, he felt an uneasy pride, as if he had an overdraft on self-respect, because he hadn't fought yet. Very late, he wondered what fighting was really like. How did it feel to be fired at? How did the enemy look? How long did it take for a crew to bale out?

Near the front the column halted. They were being split up. Wilson's troop and another were going with the squadron Second-in-Command, a worried-looking captain called Barber.

Barber didn't seem made for war. To Wilson, who knew him a little already, he seemed to belong to the easy-going atmosphere of a little Thames-side hotel, where he spent his week-ends in peacetime. Only later did he find that

62

Barber was one of the most courageous and conscientious commanders, not afraid of bringing his headquarters tank into the middle of the battle when the textbook laid down that he should have stayed to the rear.

There had been intermittent gunfire. But as they approached the sector they were to work in, it ceased. At last they pulled off the road and harboured behind a wood, while Barber went ahead to find the infantry. The troops posted guards and spread out their blankets. The enemy was half a mile away.

Just after midnight the silence was broken by a vicious little noise which went zrrrrp-zrrrrp-zrrrrp. Wilson looked at the man on guard; he wished he could ask what it was without over-emphasising his ignorance.

"Spandau," said the man. "Some poor bastard's getting it."

As he spoke, a parachute flare went up, blossoming into hard white light. For a moment everything seemed covered with a heavy frost. Then the flare floated down, leaving a trail of smoke, behind the trees.

A Bren gun fired, hard and sluggish after the Spandau. Then there was another vicious little noise.

"What's that?"

"Maybe a Schmeiser."

From across the field came the sound of a scout car. It was Barber.

"Here," he said. "I'll show you the plan for the morning."

He shone his torch on the map. Ahead of the wood were the infantry positions, and beyond them a criss-cross of fields and orchards. The infantry and a squadron of Shermans were going a thousand yards forward to take a line called "Orange." When they struck trouble the Crocodiles would go in and clear it.

63

"Better get some sleep," said Barber. "We're on call from 0500."

Wilson tried to sleep, but it was difficult. Presently someone shook him by the shoulder.

"Quarter past four, sir."

It was still dark. He buckled on his pistol belt and went round waking the crews. He didn't feel tired, but nervously alert.

A little way away someone started an engine. It groaned for a moment, then burst into life. The crews began stowing their blankets. In the turrets the operators switched on their sets. He heard his own man answering the netting call. "Item Two. O.K. Over."

Barber came out of the darkness.

"We're moving forward," he said.

Wilson watched the three long forms of the other troop's Crocodiles move across his front and tailed in behind them.

As they reached the road, the artillery started firing. The guns were positioned all round. Their flashes lit the darkness and the noise came blasting unnervingly over the hedges. Standing with his head and shoulders above the turret flaps, he felt suddenly grateful for the encircling armour and the warmth which began to seep up from the engine.

The troops moved down the road through the wood. At the end of the wood there was a misty greyness. Infantry stood by the roadside with Bren guns and rifles and mortar-bomb cases; presently they moved off, and Wilson knew that they had gone across the start line.

From time to time there were long bursts of machine-gun fire. Then there was a new noise—a long, low moaning and a succession of crumps, which he knew were mortars. They began to explode in small angry bursts among the

64

CROCODILES, TIGERS, PANTHERS

Crocodiles, and he closed the flaps, pleasantly conscious that he was now under fire and that the fire could do him no harm.

They stayed there all morning and most of the afternoon. The sounds of battle came from ahead; but wherever you looked, vision was cut off by trees and hedges. The sun was very warm. Alertness gave way to torpor. It was like a Sandhurst field day, about the time when someone said: "All right, pack up. You've just got time to get clean for dinner . . ."

Suddenly the hum in the headphones cut out. It was Barber calling them forward. They were going in to flame.

The other troop led. They ran along a path marked by tapes. Beside it was something black, swarming with flies, beneath a German camouflage cape. Further on were the first dead British.

At the start of a rise Barber was waiting with the infantry C.O. He made an up and down movement with his clenched fist, which was the sign for opening the nitrogen bottles on the trailers. Wilson jumped down.

"Got where we are?" said Barber, pointing to the place on his map. His finger moved to an orchard four hundred yards away, stayed there a moment, then moved to a field beyond it.

"There are some Spandaus there. Flame them out. The infantry will follow you. A Sherman troop's waiting to cut off the enemy at the back."

Wilson wanted to ask: How do you spot Spandaus? But it sounded too silly.

With the other troop leader he ran back to the tanks. The crews were closing the trailer doors.

"Mount!" he shouted.

They climbed in and slammed down the hatches.

65

"Driver, advance. Gunner, load H.E."

The troops moved forward in line abreast, Wilson's on the left. As they came through a hedge, mortaring started. Everywhere infantry were crouching in half-dug foxholes, trying to protect their bodies from the bursts of the bombs.

All at once it seemed to him that he'd done this before. Perhaps it was the battle course, or the flame runs at Ashford. They went through a couple of fields. Any moment now they should see the beginning of the orchard. He reached down and put on the switch which let up the fuel to the flame gun.

Suddenly it came into view: a bank of earth, another hedge, and beyond it the orchard.

"There you are. Dead ahead, driver."

The driver slammed down into second gear. The tank reared up for a moment, so that you couldn't see anything but the sky; then it nosed over the bank, and through the periscope he was looking down a long, empty avenue of trees.

Somewhere in this avenue, perhaps at the end, someone must be waiting to kill him. If only he knew what to look for.

The sergeant and corporal moved their tanks into the avenues on each side of him. The other troop started firing their machine-guns, and Wilson took the cue.

"Co-ax, fire!"

There was no target to indicate, just a patch of open field where the avenue ended a couple of hundred yards away. The gun broke into a roar, filling the turret with bitter fumes which made his eyes smart.

Through the periscope he saw the other troop start to flame, the yellow fire sweeping through the trees.

Better get his own flame going.

"Flame gun, fire!"

There was the well-remembered hiss, the slapping like leather. The fuel shot out, spraying the trees, paving the ground with a burning carpet. The tank ran on through it.

Quickly the details of the field became visible; not so much a field as a wilderness of scrub. A hundred yards to go. The forward edge was in range now.

"Slap it on, flame-gunner, all you've got!"

The flame leapt out with an almost unbroken roar. The driver was slowing up, uncertain where to go.

Suddenly the leader of the other troop called across the wireless:

"Hello, Item Two. Don't go into this lot. Let them have it from where you are!"

Wilson saw nothing but blazing undergrowth. Surely no one would have dared to stay there. But he kept the troop at the edge of the field, pouring in the flame, till the fire rose in one fierce, red wall.

Then the gun gave a splutter like an empty soda-water syphon. He looked round. The other troop had finished. They were already heading back through the smoking orchard.

He turned his own tanks and followed.

Beneath the trees with smouldering leaves, the British infantry were coming in with fixed bayonets.

Outside mortar range the troops stopped and formed up in column. Wilson opened his flaps and took off his head-set. The other troop-leader walked over the grass towards him.

"Well," he said. "That went all right."

"Sure," said Wilson. "But where were the enemy?"

"Don't worry about the enemy. All you've got to do on these jobs is to get in and flame."

Wilson did a number of actions on the same sector in the next few days. The pattern was always the same. A call to pressure up; a quick conference with the infantry; a run across some fields to flame an enemy you never saw.

Little by little he gathered opinions about the Unseen Enemy from men in the troop. Some said that as soon as the Germans saw the Crocodile trailers, they pulled out; others that they lay low, hoping that the flame would go over them. But none of them had ever seen the results of a flaming. As soon as the Crocodiles re-fuelled after action, they would be sent somewhere else.

For two days there were no casualties in the tanks.

Then, on the third day, a Sherman in a field ahead was hit by an eighty-eight. Wilson heard the slam of the shot and the rip of a Spandau. From messages on the air, he knew the enemy was shooting up the crew as they tried to bale out. A moment later a great column of black smoke billowed up, and death, which had so far been remote, seemed suddenly to take a step towards him.

The last day the troop spent on that sector, they'd just finished flaming and were coming back to re-fuel, when Wilson's tank gave a sudden lurch sideways and stopped. The final drive had gone. He sent on his other two tanks and wirelessed for the squadron A.R.V.—a turretless tank with special towing equipment.

The Crocodile lay with its tail on the edge of an enemy trench that had been overrun earlier in the morning. A little down the trench you could see a pile of bodies and the bent

68

muzzle of a Spandau. It was curious to look at those bodies, the first recognisable enemy that Wilson had seen.

His operator nudged him.

"I'll bet there's a Luger to be got off that lot."

Lugers were a great prize; every tank man wanted to get one on his belt in place of the cumbersome British .45 revolver.

When the mortaring stopped, they got out and walked along the trench. It smelled with a sweet and sickly smell, like a woman's cheap powder.

There were three bodies in the first heap. They'd been caught by a twenty-five pounder burst. One was a young N.C.O., with a hideous stomach wound. He lay half twisted on his side so that the blood had run out and congealed on the hip where he kept his pistol holster.

Wilson saw the holster first. And the operator saw that he had seen it.

"Your find, Sir."

All at once Wilson wished he hadn't come. He felt the operator looking at him, waiting to see him dig in his hand and withdraw the pistol from the mass of dark blood. In a moment it had become a matter of honour.

He bent down and pulled the body till it sat against the wall of the trench. Then, as deliberately as possible, he took the Luger from its holster and wiped the butt on a tuft of grass.

"Thanks," he said, looking at the operator. "Now find yourself one."

They went further along the trench. The dead lay everywhere. It was odd how alike they looked: all young, all with strong white teeth in mouths where the flies were gathering, all with the same golden sun-tan, now like a mask on the bloodless faces beneath. Wilson couldn't help comparing

69

them with the usual British infantry platoon, with all its mixtures which were a sergeant-major's nightmare—the tall and short, bandy-legged and lanky, heavy-limbed countrymen and scruffy, swarthy Brummagem boys with eternally undone gaiters. Even in death, he found something frightening about so much fine German manhood.

The mortaring began again. Wilson and the operator turned to go back.

Suddenly there was a shout. The gunner, who'd been left to do wireless watch, was making frantic gestures from the turret. A Spandau started firing.

They ran to the tank.

"What is it?" shouted Wilson.

"They're expecting a counter-attack."

Just then Wilson saw the front hatches open.

"Where's the driver?"

"Gone to look for loot," said the gunner, waving his hand in the general direction of the enemy.

Wilson swore.

At that moment there was a sickening moan in the air and a salvo of mortar-bombs exploded on the trench.

The driver came running across the open, and flung himself in through his open hatch.

"What the hell did you think you were doing?"

The man panted into the microphone.

"There's Jerries in the next field," he said.

Wilson felt a curious pricking at the back of his collar. The tank had its back to the enemy. He told the gunner to traverse the turret and put a new belt in the Besa.

Where had the infantry got to? Why was the recovery tank taking so long?

They waited. A Bren started firing. Spandaus broke in. Wilson picked a gap in a nearby hedge and directed the gun on it. Every second he expected to see coal-scuttle helmets, the flash of a panzerfaust.

Then he glanced back through the rear periscope, and there was the A.R.V. only ten yards away, in a field of exploding mortar bombs. Its cut-throat crew jumped out with the towing bar, and the fitter-sergeant gave Wilson a big wink.

A few minutes later the A.R.V. and the Crocodile passed back through a line of foxholes, where a platoon stood grimly behind their Bren guns. Wilson never knew what happened to them, except that the counter-attack was held. When they reached a quiet place, the fitter-sergeant came and undid the shackles.

"Thanks," said Wilson.

"All part of the service," said the sergeant. He was very pleased with himself.

Next day Wilson took over a replacement tank, and the squadron moved back to a place off the Tilly road.

V

NOYERS RIDGE

IN the new location, Wilson looked round at his fellow officers. Of the five "C" squadron troop leaders who had landed on D-Day or soon afterwards, only two were still in action. One, John Sherman, was with the squadron headquarters now. He was a neat, methodical lieutenant who on D-plus-one had organised his three Crocodiles and a section of signallers to hold off an enemy battalion for twenty-four hours.

The other was a thin, rather sensitive young man, called Grundy, who had fought on almost every part of the front. Wherever it was rumoured that the squadron was going, he would say with a sad, nervous smile: "I don't like the sound of that place—not one little bit."

The rest of the subalterns were all replacements. There was Sutherland Sherrif, a professional rugger coach called Waring, and a big, bluff Anglo-Argentinian, who'd voluntarily left a life of ease and luxury in Buenos Aires. Outside of their duties, they had little in common, and it seemed perfectly natural that all their conversation should be about the tanks and the war.

The squadron waited several days for a new operation order. Everyone felt that the last operation had been easy, and they looked towards the next with apprehension. At nights, as they lay in their bivouacs, the German artillery dropped some shells near the harbour. Every now and then

72

a shell failed to explode. The Argentinian thought it was sabotage and would call across in the dark: "There goes another load of sawdust." The rest were less buoyant. As the shelling went on, they would pull their blankets round them and try to feel closer to the earth. By day they lay in the sun, listening for the sound of the dispatch-rider's motorcycle, which would bring the order to move.

At last the order came. They were going up on a ridge towards Caen. When you climbed the ridge you could see it was an evil place. Fighting had been going on there for many days. The cornfields were flattened by shells, and in one were half a dozen burned-out Shermans. German bodies in paratroop uniform lay rotting beside the approach track, and in a clearing were some newly dead British with their boots sticking out from beneath grey blankets.

Near the top of the ridge the squadron halted and Duffy arrived from Divisional Headquarters with the plan of battle. Once again the squadron was being split up. Wilson's troop and another were going with some Shermans to lead an attack by a battalion of infantry. It was going to be a set-piece attack with a divisional artillery bombardment and all the trimmings.

He left the Crocodiles in a field, which every now and then was struck by a salvo of mortar bombs, and went with the other troop leader to find the infantry headquarters. After crawling through several hedges they found the battalion command post in a group of slit trenches. A captain took them forward to show them the ground.

The objective was a copse about five hundred yards away. But all they could see, as they lay with their bodies pressed to the earth, was the intervening waste of tall grass. Every two minutes there was a long, dismal chorus of sighs which started high in the air, came down with a wail, and ended

73

with a group of fierce explosions. It was the "sobbing sisters", a salvo from a multi-barrelled Nebelwerfer.

When they had seen what they could, they came back and briefed the crews for the attack, which was to be next morning.

The tension before a set-piece attack was appalling. When Crocodiles were used, they were generally in the lead. The timing and direction of the whole assault depended on them. You wondered if you'd done the reconnaissance properly; if you'd again recognise those small landmarks, the isolated bush, the dip in the ground, which showed you where to cross the start-line. You wondered if in the smoke and murk of the half-light battle, with your forehead pressed to the periscope pad, you'd ever pick out the target. And all the while you saw in your imagination the muzzle of an eighty-eight behind each leaf.

Wilson learned all this for the first time.

That night, because of the mortaring, the turret crews slept under their vehicles, and the drivers and co-drivers curled up in the front compartment among the controls and the big rubber fuel pipes which led to the flame-gun.

When the sentry woke him, the bombardment had already started. The troops moved into position and pressured up.

Somewhere each side in the half-light was a Sherman troop. It was a quarter of an hour to zero, and the whole thing was going to take about two and a half minutes.

The tension became almost unbearable. Then the bombardment grew louder, and the order came: "Advance."

The troop rolled forward. Wilson kept looking for his landmarks. They came up. He went on into the long grass, and there was the run with the blurred shape of the copse at the end. Spandaus were firing, but you couldn't see them. A Sherman officer was telling his troop to close up.

The distance shortened. The Crocodiles began to speed up, firing their Besas. The objective took on detail. Individual trees stood out, and beneath them a mass of undergrowth. Something slammed through the air. He knew at once that it was an anti-tank gun. But there was nothing he could do about it.

The copse was only a hundred yards away. There were gaps in the undergrowth which must surely be Spandau pits.

The troop ran in, pouring in the flame. A few yards from the trees they split up and ran along the front of the target, flaming obliquely. Whenever he saw a gap in the undergrowth he slowed down and gave it a five-second burst. Once he thought he heard screams, but it might have been the creak of the tracks on the track guides.

Suddenly it was all over. The infantry came up and ran in through the smoke. The flame-gunners put on their safety-switches, and from inside the copse came the rasp of machine-guns. A little later, when he drove back to refuel, he saw that the field was littered with dead infantry and that one of the Shermans had been hit through the turret.

Some days afterwards the squadron moved towards a place called Noyers. The division they were working with was fighting forward a few hundred yards at a time. The troops were going into action in pairs, and it was the turn of the Argentinian and Sherrif.

Squadron Headquarters and the other troops were lying under cover behind a small ridge, waiting to hear the wireless message which would mean that Sherrif and Argentine were crossing the start-line.

At last it came. For a minute there was nothing but the mush of atmospherics in the headphones and the sound of shelling and mortaring all around. Then suddenly someone shouted across the net: "Look out—in the clearing!"

Immediately there was heavy firing. It was over to the left.

The Argentinian called: "Hello Item Three . . ." But the message never finished. There was a terrific crack.

A few yards away, Duffy stood in the turret of his headquarters tank, clutching his microphone, trying to find out what had happened. But the net was jammed with a confusion of calls. The tanks were caught in the fire of a Panther, and the infantry were being cut down by Spandaus.

At last the tanks were ordered to withdraw. The artillery put down a smoke-screen, and the Crocodiles came in, one by one, across the ridge. There were only five of them. Argentine's had been hit. He had baled out with his crew, but a few yards from cover a Spandau had got them.

There were other attacks, but the enemy couldn't be moved. Towards nightfall Duffy sent a message to Division that there was a knocked-out Crocodile in no-man's-land, and the trailer hadn't caught fire.

Just before dark a rocket-firing Typhoon came over and blew it up.

Most of the time in Normandy you were fighting in a tight little box, surrounded by hedges and woods. You spent hours under mortar fire, and then you went into your box to flame. Three or four times nothing happened; then all at once one or two tanks would be hit. There were fifteen Crocodiles in a squadron and each had a crew of five. In the course of time, a good many people got killed.

Soon when Wilson went into action he thought every time of death.

It was quite against logic to suppose that you were destined to survive the war. All the appearance of things was against it. You saw a pair of boots sticking out from a blanket, and they looked exactly like your own; there was no ground for thinking that the thing that had come to the owner of these boots was not going to come just as casually to you.

When you thought about death, you developed a system of taboos. Some people lived with a lucky charm in their pocket. Wilson never carried a charm, but he had something else: an obsession that death would come as the reward for what the Greeks called "hubris".

He believed, for instance, that death would come on the first day he didn't think about it. So before going into action he would utter a phrase articulately beneath his breath: "Today I may die." It was a kind of propitiation; and yet he could never quite believe in it, because that would have defeated its purpose.

There were other forms of "hubris", like the temerity of looking at things with an eye to the future. There was the night they bombed Caen, for instance—a few days after Noyers. He looked to the east, where the bombers rumbled down through flame-reddened sky, and he listened to the dumb, distant shaking of the earth.

He thought: That's something I'll remember long after the war's over. Then he saw the danger and added in the under-breath of thought: If I survive.

At the end of July the squadron moved towards Villers Bocage.

Villers Bocage had been an objective on D-Day. British tanks had actually entered it, but had had to withdraw. Since then, battles had been fought all round, but nobody could

77

get near because of the eighty-eights. Now there was to be a big attack, preceded by an air bombardment. The Crocodiles were to mop up strong points in the wake of an armoured division.

They took up position in a field about three miles away. It was a fine, warm day, with just a little mortaring.

The R.A.F. Lancasters came over towards evening. No one was quite prepared for them. They were used to seeing daylight raids by American bombers, flying high up in faultless formation with their silver wings glittering in the sun. But the Lancasters—night-bombers—did it their own way. There was a rumble of engines as the first bunch appeared, lolloping and swaying like big black crows above the woods. They made a short circuit and went into the German flak. The bomb-doors opened and you could see the sticks of bombs falling.

The next lot came. It wasn't a formation, but more like a flying circus. They circled round and round with wing-tips almost touching, until it was their turn to go in.

As plane after plane passed over the target, the earth shook continuously and a big yellow cloud of smoke and dust arose. When the last went home, it was impossible to believe that a single German soldier was left to resist.

All around, the artillery began to fire. From the fields ahead came the sounds of battle, and the Crocodiles waited for the order to advance.

But it never came.

Just before the air raid the enemy had moved his eighty-eights well out of the town and had dug them in behind hedgerows. As the tanks of the armoured division advanced, they were caught by a deadly fire from the flanks. Dozens were destroyed outright, and those which got to cover were picked off as soon as they made any movement.

After Villers Bocage everyone grew sceptical about close support bombing. A few days later there was to be a raid on the German positions round Caen, where "B" squadron was operating.

The tanks were in action and the supply echelon was harboured a few miles back. It was commanded by a small, sad man with glasses. He had no ambition to be heroic; at Ashford, on the day he had been given the transport, he had bought Wilson a drink.

The echelon was making its evening run to the tanks' replenishing point when the bombers came over. They were American bombers, which bombed on a point to be indicated by a master navigator. Something went wrong. The first plane dropped its bombs on the convoy, and the rest followed, releasing their load on the trucks which carried petrol and nitrogen cylinders.

When they finished, "B" squadron echelon had been wiped out.

For Army and Corps headquarters the fighting in Normandy might have had a pattern, a significant development. But for the Crocodile crews it was an endless repetition of the same limited actions, varied only by the number of casualties. Among the latest was the handsome Scotsman from Eastbourne. He'd been dragged from his tank horribly burned and wasn't expected to live.

For six weeks the battle went on and on. Then all at once there was talk that the enemy was being pushed back on the Americans' front. The Americans had taken St. Lô and Avranches, and the arrows on the war maps were thrusting into Brittany.

About this time, Wilson was sent back to the regiment to collect a replacement tank. Everything at headquarters was much the same, except that there was no one left in Reserve. In the mess Drysdale told him that Dixie Dean and a young lieutenant called Beechey had been killed in "B" Squadron.

They had gone out after dark to bring back the crew of a knocked-out Sherman, but when they reached the tank, which was still burning, there was only the dead body of an infantryman on the ground. One of them touched the body and there was a violent explosion. The enemy had attached a charge to it.

Both the officers had been friends of Wilson's; for a long time he'd shared a room with one of them. But now he couldn't fix them in his mind any more. Their deaths seemed remote, like strangers'.

After lunch he took over the tank and a crew, and a young lieutenant called Macksey who was coming up to replace Argentine. The squadron was moving during the day, and he went over to the Intelligence tent to get its new location. The sergeant picked up a signal which had just come in and decoded the map-reference.

"Would you like to see it on the map, sir?"

"No thanks," said Wilson. "I'll work it out on the way. We're a bit late."

They went out on one of the "tank tracks" which had been marked out across country. Wide and straight, they cut for miles through open fields and led the tanks swiftly from the beach area to the front.

Wilson fixed the reference on his map. Apparently the squadron had been moved to a place on the far side of Villers Bocage. It didn't surprise him. In the last few days, in an attack in which the Crocodiles took no part, Villers had been taken and the war was beginning to move. All the fields which had been packed with troops and vehicles were empty. The knocked-out Panthers near the Tilly road were relics of something which had finished. It was very quiet. You couldn't even hear gunfire any longer.

The Churchill VII did thirteen miles per hour. It was twilight as they got near Villers, and dark when they entered it. There were no buildings and no streets—just a bull-dozed canyon through a pile of rubble which stretched for half a mile, and over it all the bitter taste of dust and charred wood.

The next place was called Aunay. It was just the same, except that there were some sappers there, working their bulldozer with shaded headlamps. Beyond Aunay the road went up a steep hillside, and at the top there were some infantry with anti-tank guns. Two miles further on Wilson halted the tank at a crossroads.

"This is it," he said. But there was no sign of the squadron.

They pulled the tank into the yard of a deserted farm and took it in turns to mount guard.

As soon as it was light, they pushed on cautiously to a little village which the map showed. It was eerily empty. Then a figure in a cassock appeared on the road, walking towards them. Wilson got down and went to meet him, anxious that no one should hear his stumbling French. He wondered: should he say "Father"? He wasn't a Catholic. It sounded too silly.

"Good morning, sir."

"Good morning, my son."

"Have you seen any English tanks?"

"No, my son. But I heard you arrive last night." He smiled. "The Germans also. They have just departed."

Wilson turned the tank round and they started back towards the British lines. He hoped the gunners' identification charts had been brought up to date. In case they hadn't, he reversed the turret and hung out the red-white-and-blue recognition flag.

After they had gone a mile they met the first infantry, advancing in open order astride the road. A bewildered captain held up a hand to stop them.

"Where the devil have you come from?"

Wilson told him.

The captain beckoned to his wireless operator and spoke with his battalion headquarters.

"You're luckier than you think," he said, when he'd finished. "You've just missed being at the wrong end of a divisional artillery shoot."

The squadron was in a small village at the foot of Mont Pincon when he found them. They were all very busy, getting ready to join in the general advance; there wasn't even time to tell his story, which was a pity, because it seemed to him a very good story.

The advance started off quite casually, almost in a holiday mood. They'd motor behind the infantry for two or three miles, and then there'd be a wait while the engineers put up a Bailey bridge or cleared some mines. Mostly they kept off roads and struck across country. Sometimes they'd come to a sleepy-looking village and the enemy would open up with Spandaus. There'd be a little fight, and the infantry would go in and take the village under cover of the tanks' machine-guns.

It was soon plain that the enemy had withdrawn all his armour from this area, and the infantry who were left were poor quality. At a place called Noron the squadron fired a couple of seventy-five rounds into a house and a whole company of Russian conscripts came out—heavy moujiks with patient, oriental faces. There was no flaming, but all the time the Crocodiles were held in readiness, and the crews had to keep replacing the nitrogen cylinders, which lost pressure once they were opened.

After a while they came on woods full of abandoned transport and ammunition, and curious stores like big plastic goggles, whose purpose no one knew, but which later turned out to be anti-gas goggles for horses. Everyone was talking about something called the Falaise gap.

VI

THE FALAISE GAP

UNTIL they arrived there, nobody had any idea what the Falaise gap meant. All they knew was that the remains of thirty or forty divisions—the best part of the German army in the West—were suddenly being encircled by the American advance in their rear. The only way of escape lay between Falaise and Argentan, twenty miles to the south.

One night there was a great glow in the sky. Falaise was burning. It had been captured by the Canadian army, striking out from Caen. The gap was almost closed. It became a race to stop the enemy getting out his armour.

Next day at first light the squadron moved on. The battalion they were supporting was pursuing a panic-stricken mass of infantry and transport, whom the enemy command had abandoned.

About midday there was a momentary check. The battalion came under a storm of mortar fire at a village in a close little valley between wooded hills. No one could get through. A bren-gun carrier with a load of ammunition had been hit, and the squadron waited in an orchard full of apple blossom, listening to the explosions of the burning ammunition.

Then they were called forward. The village was strewn with wreckage. The driver of the carrier was slumped over the steering-wheel like a charred sack. Wilson tried to avert his eyes, but next moment his attention was caught by a scene of almost unbelievable horror.

The village street turned into a narrow sunken road, and the road was full of dead—not British, but Germans. It was part of the column they'd been pursuing, and they'd been caught, jammed tight, in a twenty-five-pounder concentration. Men and horses were mangled and crushed in the wreckage of guns and vehicles. Some had been pressed like transfers into the earth banks beside the road. Others lay bloodily spreadeagled where the stampeding column had run over them.

There was nothing to do but to force a way through and press on. But beyond, the shambles continued. The road was blocked with the burning wreckage of motor transport. Some of the trucks had been overturned and their contents were strewn by the wayside—office stores and typewriters, crates of wine, bandages, rations, eiderdowns and suitcases.

Many of the suitcases had split open, spilling out pink women's underclothing and silk stockings. They lay on the grass among the dead, slowly being covered with a layer of ash.

All round the Falaise pocket, the same scenes were being repeated. Bridges and narrow roads were straddled with bombs and artillery fire. Dead and dying Germans formed dams where they fell in the blood-tinted rivers. No one doubted that it was the end of the war in the West.

In the evening the Crocodiles crossed an open ridge, pock-marked with abandoned trenches, and pulled up in a field where the hay had been gathered in straight, neat stacks. Duffy came and told them that the gap had been closed. They now formed part of the ring at which the enemy was expected to launch his armour in a desperate attempt to break out.

That night the blow fell, but a few miles to the south, where a Polish division of the Canadian army stood guard. The battle lasted a day and a half. The squadron was to learn of the carnage later. In one village a thousand vehicles were destroyed, and hundreds of horses stampeded into the river Dives. When it ended, the bulk of the German armour had been contained and destroyed.

The Crocodiles were put with a division which was to do the final mopping up.

While they waited for orders, the crews went out into the surrounding woods, where Duffy had given them permission to look for souvenirs.

At first they came back with the usual German helmets, which would be hung around the tank for a few days and then thrown away. Then word went round that there was better stuff to be had. The rugger coach came in with a battered Opel two-seater, and someone else with an amphibious Volkswagen. Sherrif's crew arrived, riding on a half-track. It became a kind of competitive treasure hunt. MacFarland, who was in charge of squadron transport now, came in with a big bus, painted in yellow Wehrmacht camouflage and full of Panzerfausts.

"What the hell do you think you're going to do with that lot?" said Duffy, regarding them like children on a Sunday-school treat.

"Take them along with us," said Sherrif.

"Oh no, you won't—not if the regiment knows anything about it."

"The bus would make a fine squadron office," said Mac-Farland, who knew the right approach.

Duffy thought about it.

"Let's see the thing," he said. MacFarland ran after the

bus, which a sergeant was racing round the field, still full of Panzerfausts.

"All right," said Duffy, when he'd seen the inside. "We'll take the bus. But don't go telling everyone about it."

"What about the Opel?" said the rugger coach. "It'd always be useful when the scout car's busy."

"All right," said Duffy. "Keep it hidden among the fifteen-hundredweights."

"What about the half-track?" said Sherrif. "Surely no one would mind a little half-track."

"And the Volkswagen, sir."

"All right," said Duffy resignedly. "But nothing else. Not another frigging thing."

Just then there was a heavy rumbling. Something quite enormous was pushing its way through the trees. Sergeant Pye and his fitters appeared, roaring with triumph, sitting on a Panther.

Next day, still waiting for orders, they were harboured in a field beside the road. The co-driver was cooking the midday meal over the petrol stove.

"What's it today—stew again?" said Wilson.

The co-driver grinned, making a great mystery. "Wait and see," he said.

At last the meal was ready. The co-driver wiped out the mess-tins with a swab of cotton-waste from his pocket and filled them with small lumps of meat, swimming in a rich white sauce. Everyone took a spoonful.

"Like it?"

It was delicious. It turned out to be German tinned rabbit.

In the afternoon, the squadron was called to clear out a battalion of paratroopers who were caught in the trap and refused to surrender. Duffy sent Wilson and Grundy ahead in the scout car to meet the infantry. The squadron followed with its curious additions to the transport echelon. Someone said afterwards that it broke the fitters' hearts to leave the Panther.

On the way there were many dead cows: the infantry were shooting up the inflated carcasses with Sten-guns, so that they burst and allowed the nauseous gasses to escape. Suddenly Wilson felt sick, but it wasn't an ordinary sickness. He felt a violent twisting in his guts. Presently he stopped the car and vomited.

At the rendezvous an infantry captain was waiting. He was distressingly cheerful. When they went forward and started to discuss the ground, Wilson had to break off and disappear behind a hedge. He came back trembling, with a curious chill all over him.

"Are you all right?" said the captain.

"It's nothing," said Wilson. But as the captain went on to explain the plan of attack, the pains gripped his stomach more and more fiercely, and to look at the map made him giddy.

"Zero seventeen-hundred hours," said the captain.

They went back to the road and waited for the squadron. Wilson could hardly stand now. When the squadron arrived, Grundy passed on the plan to Duffy and they mounted their tanks.

"Anything wrong, sir?" said the operator.

Wilson shook his head, but he had to keep pressing his stomach against the edge of the cupola to deaden the pain. The next thing he knew was that the column had stopped and he was being helped down to the ground.

"Good God," said the co-driver. "Have I poisoned you, sir?"

"Pick you up on the way back," said the troop sergeant.

The tanks drove off. He was lying in the middle of a field. The enemy had started to mortar, and he was being sick again. A little way off he could see the spoil where someone had dug a slit trench. Several times he tried to crawl towards it, but the pains in his stomach held him motionless.

For a long time he lay with his face to the ground, with the fumes from the exploding mortar bombs drifting all around him. Then the squadron was coming back.

"Pick him up," said someone. It was the troop corporal.

"Where's the sergeant?"

"Went on a mine, sir. The tank brewed up but they all baled out."

Everything faded. Then he was being taken into an aid post and someone was putting pills into his mouth.

"Dysentery," said an M.O.

VII

GUNS AT GRIS NEZ

IT was business-like and clean in the Field Hospital. You could feel the spread of sunlight on the canvas roof of the marquee, and white-coated orderlies kept passing with bed-pans and bottles.

In the next bed was a German lieutenant. He'd just had his leg off and all day and night he kept moaning.

"Can't you keep the bastard quiet," said someone. But the orderlies shook their heads. The German was supposed to have a blood transfusion, but he wouldn't allow it. After some days he got very weak, and they fixed in a tube while he was unconscious.

There were two middle-aged Englishwomen in Red Cross uniform, who came round each day with cigarettes. Their routine was to visit the American hospital across the road picking up crisp, cellophaned packets of Chesterfields. They gave them to the British officers in exchange for issue Woodbines, which they then took to the other ranks' hospital.

There was a beautiful ward sister. But dysentery was so unromantic that Wilson felt embarrassed when she came near his bed. He envied the infantry officers at the far end of the tent, who at least had honest wounds.

After some days the German began to recover. He'd commanded a company of anti-tank guns.

"Eighty-eights?" said Wilson.

The German nodded. They both grinned, and Wilson wondered how many Churchills he'd knocked out.

After that the German talked a lot. He was thinking all the time of what he'd do when he got home and he got out pictures of his fiancée—a pretty, dark-haired girl in a little town in Bavaria.

The other officers resented having the German. One of them was a Canadian captain. Once, when the sister was out of the ward, he told how he'd been sent to search a cornfield and found a pair of Germans hiding in a foxhole. "Where are the rest?" he'd asked. But the Germans wouldn't answer. He shot one with his pistol, and then the other led him to the rest of the section. When they came out, he shot the lot.

Wilson didn't much like the German: it was disconcerting to talk with someone for whom the war had already ended. But after this he talked with him more than he might otherwise have done.

At last Wilson was discharged. He was glad. News had come in that the regiment was going into battle at the Channel ports. He picked up his kit to walk over to the depôt which sent people up to the front again. The German said goodbye with many tears, embarrassingly—for it was impossible to forget what the S.S. had done to Harvey.

Before you could get back to your unit, you had to pass through a Delivery squadron. He was sent to a Delivery squadron which was far away from the war, in a field near Rouen. There were lines of brown tents, a couple of cooking stoves, and a wireless which just failed to reach the regiment's Divisional Headquarters forty miles away.

Every few days drafts arrived at the Delivery squadron, but none seemed to leave. It lacked only barbed wire to make it a prison camp.

Wilson shared a tent with a Regular Army lieutenant just out from England called Dunkley. He had spent the war training with some special equipment for a secret operation, which had to be called off. Now he was waiting to be posted to Crocodiles. He was very bitter. But for the cancelled operation, he would have been a captain; and he put all his anger into a curious, clipped use of the word "chum". "Wasted the last four years, chum; and now I suppose I'll spend the rest of the war in this dump."

Each morning after queuing in the rain for breakfast, they would go to the Commandant to ask when they could go to the regiment; and the Commandant would ease back his well-fed body in a frail canvas chair and tell them they must wait for posting orders. In the afternoons they would walk across the fields to a lonely estaminet, where peasants played dominoes. There, drinking Calvados, they would share their despair and plot ways of escape.

On the tenth day, Wilson could stand it no longer. After breakfast he wrote the Commandant a letter, asking him to excuse the informality of not saying goodbye. He gave the letter to his batman with orders to give it to the Commandant in two hours. Then he took the haversack which Dunkley had packed with his own chocolate and cigarette ration, and slipped out.

On the road to Boulogne he stopped a truck. After they'd gone a little way the driver said: "Of course, you've got a movement order?"

"Of course," said Wilson. "Do you want to see it?"

"No," said the driver. "You look pretty genuine."

Then he told the story of the Deserters' Transit Camp.

According to this story two quartermasters had set themselves up in a farmhouse near the Normandy beaches. There, from time to time, they received other ranks and sold them fake passes to take them home to England on the landing-ships. After a while, it became a regular camp. They collected rations with fake requisition forms and lorries stolen from a transport dump. They even invented a fake Brigade Sign. It was only discovered when a passing general had a motor breakdown and asked them to send for the Brigade R.E.M.E.

Wilson reflected that under military law he, too, was a deserter now. He wondered what the penalty was, and how long it would be before the regiment knew.

The truck took him to the edge of Boulogne and stopped.

"Sorry, sir. This is as far as I can take you."

He lifted his kit out of the back and crossed the canal by a rough foot-bridge.

He'd known Boulogne before the war—a busy little place with red-brick houses you watched from the train window. But this wasn't Boulogne.

He walked through the empty streets. Sometimes the houses were shells, and sometimes just piles of rubble. On one blackened wall he saw the silver flame-thrower slime; you couldn't mistake it.

Just as he was despairing of meeting anyone, he saw a sergeant in a jeep.

"Hi!" he shouted.

The man looked round. It was a Signals sergeant from the regiment.

"Hello, sir. What are you doing here?"

"Looking for a lift. I'm just back from hospital. What are *you* doing?"

"I'm looking for the National Provincial Bank."

He had worked for the bank in peace time. It had had a branch in Boulogne and he wanted to see what was left of it.

Wilson climbed into the jeep, and they drove up through

the strange, empty town on the road where the signs said
Calais. At the top of the hill the jeep slowed down and they
looked across the water.

"We ought to see England," said the sergeant. "But it's
not very clear today."

We ought to see England. . . .

Three months ago (it seemed much longer) they had
landed in Normandy, the last place anyone thought of.
They'd fought in those strange fields and orchards, till
Normandy with its rotting cows and charred tanks had
become their accepted environment. Now they'd come
round to the coast where it once seemed that everything
should have started.

"Where's 'C' squadron?" said Wilson.

"On the cliffs above Calais," said the sergeant.

"Has anyone got into the town yet?"

"They're expecting to get it tonight."

"And after that?"

"Cap Gris Nez. The cross-channel guns. They've left
them till last."

They were running down the hill towards Marquise.
The sea was out of sight. The ground sloped up on the left
towards the headland.

"How about those guns—can they fire inland?"

As if in answer to Wilson's question, there was a distant
boom, and a house on the edge of the village dissolved in a
cloud of smoke.

"Damn," said the sergeant. "We'll have to take the road
round the back."

That evening Wilson got a truck from the regiment and
went off with the supply echelon. They followed a narrow
track up the back of the cliffs, where every turning had a
notice saying "Beware—Mines."

There was ragged firing. Rain was blowing in from the sea. As the convoy came up to the top it reached the rim of a big semi-circular depression. Calais lay eastwards, Cap Gris Nez to the left. All round the cliffs were the fires of burning buildings, flaring red in the wind, so that the whole scene was like something from a nineteenth-century battle picture— the night after Waterloo perhaps, or the retreat from Moscow.

The convoy edged forward. At a fork in the track there was a notice with a big red arrow and the one word "Enemy". They pulled off into a dip, and there were the dark forms of the Crocodiles.

Wilson jumped off the truck and went in search of his troop. He found his corporal's crew stowing fresh ammunition. But the troop didn't exist any more. It had been broken up and used to replace other people's casualties. He went to look for Duffy.

"Hello," said Duffy. "Recovered?" That was all. He seemed very tired.

Just then Grundy came up.

"You've come at the right time," he said. "You can do the frigging patrol tonight."

"What patrol?"

"Looking for a better firing position."

"Yes," said Duffy. "You can do that."

Grundy took Wilson aside and showed him the map. Just beyond the dip where they stood were enemy pill-boxes and mines. Grundy himself had been out the night before. He'd stumbled into a pill-box and shot up some German sentries. Now he was nursing an enormous bump on his head, where a dud grenade had hit him.

The patrol was to go out at ten. They waited in the shelter of Grundy's tank, and he told Wilson about all the squadron had been doing.

95

In Boulogne they had lost another replacement officer. It was his first action. Later Macksey had run into trouble. His Crocodile had been hit at a street intersection, and he'd baled out with a smashed arm and hidden in a drain. Then he realised that his driver was still aboard. But before he could go back and get him, the tank rolled forward of its own accord and came under fire from an eighty-eight and some Spandaus. It started to brew up. For a minute the driver screamed, till the flames swept forward and engulfed him.

For the past two days the squadron had been sitting on the heights, having a long-range gun-fight with a battery of 40mm anti-aircraft guns on the Calais perimeter. The tank carrying Grundy's sergeant had been hit fourteen times, but the shots hadn't penetrated.

Wilson and Grundy talked on in the dark and the rain. Then about 9.30 Duffy came and said the patrol was "off" for some reason. Wilson was glad; he'd never had the least idea what he was supposed to do on it.

Next day Calais was taken. The squadron moved back to Marquise to get ready for the assault on Cap Gris Nez, and Wilson took over Grundy's troop, because Grundy was wanted as permanent Reconnaissance Officer.

Whenever an officer of the rank of colonel upwards had to give an order for a tricky operation, there was a technique which never failed. He had only to lead off with some phrase such as "Now, gentlemen, we're going to clear up a couple of Panzer divisions", or (as it was to be later) "You and I are going to crack the Siegfried Line", and everyone saw that to worry about little things like eighty-eights was small-minded.

It was a Canadian colonel who issued orders for the assault on the Channel guns.

"Well, gen'l'men, you'll see from the map that we're going for two separate batteries up there. The one on the west is fixed to fire on the English coast. The eastern battery has 360 degrees traverse. We're taking the east: it's got four guns, but a couple are out of action."

When he came to "any questions", someone asked: "Excuse me, sir, but how big are the guns?"

Everyone laughed. The colonel smiled a little. The question seemed rather academic.

"I guess they're fifteen inchers."

Wilson looked round the smoke-filled room. There were the infantry company commanders and an artillery major and a number of officers of the Engineers. From his own division there were mild, un-military-looking men, who commanded an array of curious machines for blowing up mines, crossing craters and blowing holes through fifteen-foot thicknesses of concrete.

"Christ," said the rugger coach, as they came out into the daylight: "All we've got to do is to drive the Crocodiles up the ruddy gun-barrels."

They went back to the squadron for lunch, and in the afternoon a Canadian officer collected them to take them to the "peep-hole".

The peep-hole was a deserted farmhouse rather forward on the edge of some high ground looking towards the guns. They climbed a ladder to a door in the attic. A couple of Canadians were sitting in armchairs, taking it in turns to look through a pair of giant binoculars, which they ranged across the countryside through a hole in the tiles.

"Keep well back," said one of the Canadians. "You can see all you want from behind me."

Wilson stood back with the others and scanned the

ground. Everything was startlingly clear—the big square cupolas of the guns, the concrete of the casemates and blockhouses, the yellow spoil from trenches. Away on the left were the roofs of a deserted village. The whole terrain was pock-marked with bomb craters. Nothing moved. The only sound was the talk of the Canadian look-outs.

Suddenly there was a terrific slam. Something came in through the roof and went out the other side. The Canadians jumped out of their chairs and pushed their visitors towards the exit. Methodically the eighty-eight removed the roof.

The guard called him in the morning, while it was still dark. He reached out for his beret, which had shrunk in the dew, and buckled on his belt. Then they warmed up the engines and made a quick breakfast of tea and bread and margarine.

No one spoke much: they were all subdued by their own private thoughts—except for one man, the gunner in the sergeant's crew. He was a heavy-looking, red-faced boy, who normally spoke little. But now he kept going among the crews, making unheeded little jokes about this being the great day. He came from Dover and his family had lived under fire from the guns for nearly four years.

The squadron moved out at first light. Sherrif and another troop went first; they were going in with the assault on the western battery. As soon as they were out, Wilson took 14 Troop to a ridge behind the peep-hole and waited.

In the mist, other vehicles were assembling. Just ahead was a troop of AVREs. Wilson knew what they were now; a version of the Churchill without the seventy-five. Instead they had a little spigot projecting from the turret, on which was fitted something like a dustbin, full of explosive. He hadn't seen them in action yet, but he knew that when they came up to a pill-box they fired the dustbin at point-blank range.

There were other AVREs, carrying fascines—great bundles of brushwood, twice as high as the vehicle itself, held to the front by wire ropes. When the time came, the ropes would be cut by guncotton, and the bundles would roll into streams or craters to make a crossing for the tanks.

Then there were the Flails—Sherman tanks with revolving drums and chains attached to them, which beat the ground and exploded mines as they went along. And a thing called a Conga—a Bren carrier loaded with nitroglycerine. When it reached a minefield, it was supposed to shoot a hose across and pump it full of liquid explosive. Then it would explode the hose, and the mines with it.

There were many other things, but Wilson couldn't see them. All the armour was forming up in a column; first the Flails with an infantry company, then the Crocodiles, then the fascines and the other devices. The British artillery had been firing since dawn, but not yet the German.

At seven o'clock the column went over the ridge. For a moment they saw the big square outlines of the guns again, and beyond them, clear in the morning air, a strip of sea and the sunlit roofs of Dover. Next moment the column was running down into a little valley. The view was cut off, and machine-guns started firing.

At the bottom of the valley the column stopped. The infantry had suddenly gone to ground. Something was firing from a pill-box on the far slope, and everyone had their guns trained on it. Presently the armour started moving again, firing at the pill-box. There were still no mines, but there was a small stream at the bottom. One of the Flails nosed into it and got stuck.

99

There was a call on the wireless for fascines. An AVRE came lumbering by from its place in the column. It went down to the stream and blew the charges securing the brushwood. But something went wrong; the bundle didn't spread out. The crew had to dismount and begin breaking up the bundle by hand.

Wilson left his gunner firing at the pill-box and went down to help. The ground by the stream was waterlogged, and the AVRE crew were sweating and floundering in a mass of sticky clay. It was going to take too long. He went back to the turret, which was shaking with the racket of firing, and beckoned to the operator. The operator raised himself, his headphones clamped over his ears and his eyes streaming with the cordite fumes from the Besa.

"Tell them to send down some people from the other crews," Wilson shouted.

The operator nodded. Just then a bullet struck the flap of the cupola, sending off a shower of sparks between them. The operator looked surprised and ducked down. Next minute Wilson heard him calling over the net.

After a while the crews got the brushwood spread and as the Flails and Crocodiles went over the stream, a section of infantry crept up on the pill-box with sticky-bombs and grenades.

The ground on the far side was nothing but craters—a moonscape in yellow clay. The Flails began the ascent, thrashing with their chains. Almost at once they got ditched. A troop of Canadian Shermans appeared and overtook them. They went up the ridge out of sight. There was a lot of mortaring and a couple of heavy explosions. As Wilson came up, he saw one of the Shermans nose-down in a crater. The other two had their tracks off.

There was also the Conga. He had no idea how it had

got there. The driver was racing and bucking it, to get it out of a deep rut. The liquid nitro-glycerine needed only one hard knock to explode it, and you could almost hear it swilling and splashing in the tanks. The Crocodiles gave the Conga a wide berth. They were in the lead now.

It was heavy going. There was still no sign of the big guns, but you knew they were waiting at the top of the crest. The Crocodiles with their heavy trailers strained in bottom gear. It took a minute to cover ten yards. The engines were fast over-heating. Every time they paused to negotiate a way between craters a wave of heat would drift up from the air louvres. And all the time Duffy was calling from behind to know how far they had got.

The main thing was to avoid mines. The bombing had blown most of them up, but wherever there was a yard or two of undisturbed soil the mines were sure to be under the surface. There was no guessing the exact spot. You could only drive on and hope that the tank tracks would go between them. There was a great deal of machine-gunning. The infantry were nowhere to be seen. Perhaps they were dealing with the three or four eighty-eights which had been reported.

"Driver right, driver left—hold her steady—there's a steep drop coming . . ."

Gradually Wilson lost all sense of time and distance. The big guns might be only two hundred yards away—or they might be a quarter of a mile. Then suddenly his tank reared up over a bank of clay. Immediately in front was a vast wall of steel and concrete. It was only when he looked up and saw the enormous gun-barrel hanging over him that he realised that he had reached the battery.

Over to the left were the other guns, grey, square and motionless. There was no recognised drill for dealing with a battleship on land. There seemed nothing to do but dismount.

There was a great deal of noise. This was the middle of the enemy's fortress, and a ragged battle was going on all around.

"Shall I come too?" said the operator.

They walked up to the concrete platform, clutching their pistols. At the front there was no way of climbing it, so they went round to the back, where bombs had heaped up the earth. They managed to scramble up.

There was a narrow door in the side of the steel cupola. Wilson tried the handle. To his amazement it moved, and the door swung outwards. In the dim shaft of daylight he picked out the mechanism of the gun—the open breech, a great shell lying in a cradle, a platform of steel plates. There was a heavy smell of oil.

He shouted. He wasn't sure what he should shout, but the thing was to make it sound aggressive.

His words echoed back, hollow and theatrical. "Come on out of it!"—and he realised he was standing on the edge of a shaft which went deep into the ground.

He waited for the echo to die. Then everything was silent, except for the muffled noise of the battle outside.

He shouted again.

Presently, from far below, he heard the sound of boots on an iron ladder. They were coming up, taking an endless time about it. At first there seemed to be only one pair. Then he made out several.

At last, from almost by his feet, a face appeared. Then came others. They were all very scared. One was a corporal. As he came out he reached into his pocket and thrust something with sharp edges into Wilson's hand.

"You take it. I don't want it," he said in English.

It was an Iron Cross.

When Wilson had the prisoners outside, he saw that the
infantry had arrived. They were standing round the other
guns, and other groups of prisoners were coming out, with
hands raised, from the steel doors. All the concrete emplacements seemed to have opened up, except one: a concrete
block-house, which Wilson hadn't noticed before. Sappers
were busy on it, fixing a big charge of explosive called a
Beehive.

Suddenly one of Wilson's prisoners saw it too. He began
to make frightened gestures.

"What is it?"

The man spoke no English, but beckoned Wilson
frantically to come into the cupola again. They went in.
The man pointed to the shell which was lying in the cradle
and then began opening and closing his fingers, as one does
when one indicates a number.

It was obviously a very great number.

"All right," said Wilson. "I'll tell them."

No one seemed certain what was to happen next. There
was still some mortaring. Perhaps it came from the German
fire-control station, which lay about a mile away, by the
edge of the cliffs. After a while the mortaring slackened.

Barber came up in his support tank.

"What now, Derek?"

"Lunch," said Barber.

"Lunch?"

"Sure. Everything stops for lunch with the Canadians."

They pulled up the Crocodiles behind an earth bank,
and the crews cooked tins of steak and kidney pudding on
their petrol cookers. While they ate, they sat on the bank
and looked across at the fire-control station, which they
were going to take in the afternoon. It was a concrete

structure, like a ship's bridge, surrounded by block-houses and trenches. Every now and then a stray shot sailed over.

At two o'clock Barber came with the order to go on. It was to be Crocodiles only from now, because the Flails couldn't take the ground.

Wilson led the troop down into another little valley, with the infantry spread out on either side. The ground was marked on the map as a minefield, but most of the mines had been exploded. When they reached the bottom, they came to the remains of a road and some houses. Suddenly there was an explosion. Wilson looked round and saw that his corporal's tank had its track off. The corporal—a happy little East End tailor called Grossman—waved him on.

They followed the road, creeping between the houses, firing the seventy-fives into everything which might hide danger. Then the road ran up a little slope, and all at once they were looking across a couple of hundred yards of bomb-torn clay at the final objective.

There was a line of freshly turned earth, a zig-zag of trenches; and beyond that the block-houses and the "ship's bridge".

"Fire an air-burst," said Wilson.

The operator set the fuse screw in the side of the shell and tapped the gunner's arm.

The gun slid violently back and the shell exploded above the trenches in a puff of smoke and flame.

"Repeat."

Suddenly in the trenches a German was waving a strip of white cloth.

Wilson looked round. The infantry hadn't appeared yet.

"All right," he said. "This is where we walk."

The operator and co-driver got out and followed him. They stumbled across the craters, past a big yellow board

with a skull and cross-bones and the German gothic letter-
ing "Achtung Minen".

Somewhere on the left, someone fired a machine-gun.
Then Wilson realised that whoever it was, was firing in
another direction, and the distance to the trenches seemed a
little shorter.

As they approached, a number of figures appeared in
the trenches. At first there were a dozen, then about a
hundred: they had thrown away their arms and even their
helmets.

"Who speaks English?" said Wilson.

An N.C.O. came forward.

"Where is your commander?"

"I will take you."

Wilson left his crew to gather and guard the prisoners
and followed the N.C.O. They went towards a block-house,
scarred with bombs and perhaps with shells from the
English guns across the straits. From its doorway a German
officer came to meet them, wearing a tall peaked cap and
with the badges of a naval *Kapitän-Leutnant* on his greatcoat. He looked about fifty.

The N.C.O. saluted and exchanged a few words with
the officer. "The commander would like to collect some
personal belongings before you take him away," he said.

"Does the commander speak French?"

The *Kapitän-Leutnant* nodded.

Wilson dismissed the N.C.O. and went with the commander into the block-house.

There was no electricity any more, and the place was lit
with candles. They went down a long spiral staircase. In
the bunk at the bottom was a divan, a table, an open chest-
of-drawers full of clean linen. Smoke was filtering through
a crack in the concrete wall.

"Where does that come from?"

"From the wireless room. It's been burning since yesterday."

The *Kapitän-Leutnant* took a small canvas grip from a cupboard and packed it with shirts and socks. Then he went over to the table and picked up a photograph of his wife. It was a large photograph, and when it would not go into the grip, he took it from the frame and with a tired, despairing gesture ripped it into small pieces.

"I'm ready now," he said.

But at that moment, as if at a prearranged signal, a batman appeared from some dark, unexpected recess. He carried a tray with two glasses and a bottle of Benedictine.

"Please," said the *Kapitän-Leutnant*. And in the gloom of the smoke-filled bunker they solemnly drank each other's health.

Out in the daylight, the infantry had arrived and were taking over the prisoners. It had started to rain—a cold, fine sea-rain, which stung the face and dripped from the peaks of the Germans' service caps.

Wilson took the commander away and handed him over to a major. Then he walked back down the hill, towards the tanks. It was very silent. He was thinking what a fantastic day it had been, and how the Canadian colonel had had every right to be blasé about the guns. Half-way across the minefield he came on the twisted wreck of a Bren carrier with a little crowd round it. It was the Canadian colonel's, and he was dead.

VIII

ZERO AT ROSMALEN

You never quite knew where you were with Duffy: just when you thought you'd done something clever, you found that you'd annoyed him. Partly the trouble was that Duffy wanted always to be in minute control of everything that went on in his squadron—and in action that wasn't possible.

On the other hand, troop leaders like Wilson would often try to trick Duffy by little devices of wireless procedure. Thus, when they had something in mind which Duffy was sure to forbid, they would not use the proper procedure: "Hello X, I'd like to do so and so, Over." Instead they'd say: "Hello X, I'm doing so and so, Out." And generally, before Duffy could recover himself, someone else would come up with a message and block the air.

Something like this had happened when Wilson dismounted and went up to the fire-control station, and Duffy was in a mean temper.

"Did you cut yourself off deliberately?" he asked.

"Well, sir, not exactly. I thought you might have been busy. . . ."

"That, my dear Wilson, is beside the point. What I want's a straight answer. Frigging yes, or frigging no?"

"Frigging yes, sir."

Duffy stood there for a moment, his small moustache twitching with fury, and then he turned on his heel.

"Now you've done it," said Sherrif.

But an hour later, when the troop leaders went to Duffy's bivouac to get some orders, Duffy was in a genial mood. He passed round a bottle of whisky. The C.O., he said, had been very pleased with the action at Cap Gris Nez. So had he. Now they'd have a few days' rest.

When the group was dispersing, Duffy caught Wilson's eye.

"Frigging yes or frigging no?" he said with a grin.

"Frigging yes, sir."

After that it became a kind of countersign between them.

Wilson was relieved that the business with Duffy had passed over, because there was something else coming up, and he might need his help.

After four days, when it seemed unbelievable that nothing had happened, the message arrived: "You're wanted at regimental headquarters."

The regiment was harboured on a rain-swept hill a mile or so from the now-silent guns. He found the Adjutant working in his tent beneath dripping trees. He was not unfriendly, but he was subject, as are all Adjutants, to a horror of anything irregular. As he looked up, there was almost pity in his face.

"We had a letter from the Delivery squadron," he said. "What on earth made you do it?"

He led Wilson to the C.O.'s tent next door.

"Wilson's here, sir."

"Show him in."

Waddell sat behind a table. He was utterly cold.

"Well, Wilson, ye're in serious trouble," he said. "I'll show ye the Squadron Commander's letter, and maybe ye'll tell me if what he says is correct."

Wilson took the letter and read it.

"Yes, sir. It's correct, but it doesn't say everything."

"How?"

"There's no mention that I'd been waiting ten days before I did this."

"Ten days?"

"Yes, sir. The Squadron Commander said he couldn't send me up till you called for me."

Waddell looked surprised and wrote something on a pad.

"Were there any others there from the regiment?"

"Yes."

"All right. Tell me more about this Delivery squadron." There was a faint acidity about the word "delivery" as Waddell pronounced it.

When Wilson had finished, Waddell looked up.

"Well," he said. "I'll try to keep it from going any further. At least ye went in the right direction."

As Wilson came out of the C.O.'s tent, he saw William Douglas Home: he had his back towards him and was walking down the lines with a strange officer at his side.

"I'll just go over and see him," said Wilson.

"I wouldn't just now," said the Adjutant. "He's under arrest."

Even when he sailed with the regiment to Normandy, William had continued his private war-against-war. While headquarters were near Bayeux, he had written to the newspapers about some German ambulances shot up by British fighters. And what he had written was true. Wilson had seen the ambulances, riddled with bullets on the Tilly road.

Later Waddell had posted William to Duffy's squadron to take part in the assault on Le Havre. There were thousands of civilians in the town, which was soon to be bombed with 50,000 tons of explosive. William's moment of

decision had at last arrived. On the morning of the battle
he returned to regimental headquarters and, finding the C.O.
in the act of shaving, told him that he refused to take part.
Waddell called a witness.

"Will you carry out my order, Home?"—"No, sir."

The three Crocodiles which Wilson inherited from
Grundy were called "Supreme, "Sublime" and "Superb".

"Supreme" was the troop-leader's. The driver was a
quiet, fatherly man, who went into battle as phlegmatically
as if he were driving a bus. When he came out, he spent
hours trying to straighten damaged headlamps and track
guards. The co-driver was a cheeky Welshman called
Randall, who when he wasn't arguing with Wilson, was
constantly at war with the gunner and the wireless-operator.

The troop sergeant was a young man called Warner.
Unobtrusive, quiet-spoken, Warner was the indispensable
type of N.C.O., who achieved everything by his example,
who in battle was always where he was needed. Once, when
he had temporarily to surrender his place to allow a reserve
sergeant to gain experience, Wilson saw him almost on the
verge of tears.

The rest of the crews were a mixture of Cockneys,
Midlanders and Scots, known only by their nicknames, like
"Ticker", "Nobby" and "Jock". It was a very happy troop.
Most of them were under twenty-four.

While the squadron was waiting to move a new officer
arrived. It was Dunkley, who had at last escaped from the
Delivery squadron. He took over the troop which had
belonged in turn to Benzecry, Argentine and Macksey.

Then the transporters came, and they set off on the long
road through Belgium. They passed sign-posts with names
from another war—Poperinghe, Passchendaele, Menin,

Ypres. The long straight ribbon of Napoleonic pavé was lined with the wrecks of German transport, and all the time they were passed by other convoys bringing up supplies and ammunition to the front in Holland.

Late on the third night they reached Bourg-Leopold and off-loaded the tanks for a road march. What they had seen of Belgium had been outwardly untouched by the war; but as soon as they reached the Dutch border they smelled the familiar smells of dead cows and the burned thatch of unseen buildings. The ground was very flat. There was a silvery mist; and all along the empty road which stretched northwards, you had the feeling you were travelling on an endless dyke.

The squadron was sent to a place called Winssen to the West of Nijmegen. At first the farm at Winssen looked forbidding. It stood on the edge of a cheerless marsh, and the rain and wind which blew across the polder beat hard on the flaking paint of the doors.

When they arrived the old man went all round his barn chalking up his only words of English: "No smokes." Then, as they settled in, he lost a little of his anxiety. His wife released their copper-haired daughters, who were hidden in the kitchen, and invited the officers to warm themselves by the stove.

The front was all around. To the east was Germany; to the west a big enemy pocket which reached to the sea; to the north a desolate stretch of heavily-shelled ground called "the island".

Once they went into the island, which one reached through Nijmegen. The town was in the front line. In the streets were big smoke canisters, which were set alight whenever the enemy started shelling. The great steel bridge was guarded by Royal Engineers, who watched for mines which the Germans were floating down the river. Fire engines waited in the streets to put out fires which the shells started, and all the time the remaining civilians were going about their business.

One evening, shortly after they had been into the island, Duffy told them they were going to clear out part of the pocket to the south-west. The officers were sitting in the farmhouse parlour, which had now become the mess. One of the daughters was playing a mandolin. There was a crackle of wood in the stove, a bottle of Bols on the table, and the patter of rain on the blacked-out windows.

Wilson went out to warn his troop for the move. They were sitting, half-soaked, in the lee of a truck, trying vainly to light a stove to brew tea.

It wasn't anyone's fault: there was simply nowhere else for them to go. But suddenly he saw the frightening difference between the officers' war and the men's—how everything, from the award of honours to the warmth of a stove, fell to the officers, while it was taken for granted that the men should bear their part with regimental pride.

From then on he felt increasingly uneasy whenever the squadron was concentrated. He clung to the days when he could live, eat and sleep with his crew.

Next morning the squadron left on the road to 'sHertogenbosch. It was a fine day with a touch of autumn in the air. For a while they ran through the quiet countryside. Then they heard the sound of guns and turned off the road where a knocked-out Sherman stood facing an abandoned anti-tank gun.

The ground was held very thinly here. The squadron stopped by some cottages and a woman told them that the enemy came round in the night, foraging for bicycles.

The crews not on guard spent the night in a hayloft, and next morning the squadron joined up with a squadron of Cromwells from an armoured brigade, which had been probing the enemy's defences. They made a common harbour in two adjacent fields. Away to the east, across the flat countryside, you could see the broken spire of Rosmalen church, with an even round shell hole in what once was the belfry. The enemy had a look-out there.

Wilson met the Lancers' Sergeant-Major. "What's the form?"

The sergeant-major winked. "Watch haystacks," he said. "They've got a habit of changing position."

They were to attack Rosmalen next morning. In the afternoon Barber came back from an infantry battalion order group and told the troop leaders to go up and do a reconnaissance.

They found a lonely company dug in behind a hedge.

"O.K.," said the Company Commander. "Keep your heads down and follow me."

They crawled along a ditch, which struck out into no man's land. The mortars were crumping gently a little way down the line, and somewhere a Spandau zipped. Now and then, as they worked their way forward, a bird would fly up.

"There you are," said the Company Commander. "The village is in the trees. The red roof by the church is what we call the Rectory. There's some sort of anti-tank gun to the left, and a bit of a stream in the dead ground just before it. O.K.?"

"O.K.," said Wilson.

They crawled back faster than they came. The mortars were ranging on them, hitting the ditch and throwing up clods of earth.

Wilson fell asleep, wondering what kind of gun it was by the Rectory. He was sure that death, when it came, would be from an anti-tank gun. He saw in his mind's eye the muzzle of the gun as it moved behind the leaves of some bush or in a shadowy space between buildings. He had learned the aspect of every gun by heart. It had a certain advantage: it made him almost indifferent to shelling.

Someone pressed his shoulder and said "Reveille." He looked at the luminous dial of his watch: it was four-fifteen. He put on his belt and beret and picked up his map-case.

The darkness was absolute. A breeze swept the harbour, cold and edged with rain. Around the vehicles the first shadowy figures were moving, opening up and stowing away the blankets. An hour to zero. At any moment now the five-fives would open up. He waited in the shelter of his tank.

At the fixed moment the sky to the rear was lit with a sheet of flame, and the earth shook gently beneath him. He stood listening. From high in the darkness came the long, fluttering thrum of the shells. He strained to look east-wards, away beyond the village where the enemy's support line ran.

Two, three, four seconds passed. He was aware of other figures round him, which had stopped whatever they were doing and were looking eastwards too. But all that came back was a deep, protracted rumbling of the ground.

"All right," he said. "Get mounted."

In the turret the operator was answering the netting call. Dunkley came up on the air, and then Sherrif, reporting their troops ready to move. A moment later a dozen long shapes came looming through the darkness and went clanking out of the harbour. It was the Lancers.

The squadron followed. They moved slowly. Sometimes there was the exhaust-glow of the tank in front to follow, and sometimes only a cloud of dust. Down below the gunner was asleep, his head lolling against Wilson's legs. He was a funny little country lad, and the others were always teasing him because he was so scruffy and tongue-tied. Wilson wondered if he dreamed down there, and if so, what. It was always the gunner who got out last when a tank brewed up.

Suddenly the Lancers stopped. It was the forming-up point.

Wilson and the co-driver dismounted and opened up the valves on the trailer. Outside the tank, away from the hum of the headphones, there was a world of noise and death. The enemy was shelling along the start-line, and every now and then something solid and heavy slammed through the air. You couldn't mistake an anti-tank gun. This one was firing blind, perhaps at the sound of the engines.

They re-mounted, and Wilson looked at his watch. He thought of the dials in the trailer, which would still be going up, showing the rising pressure of the nitrogen on the fuel tanks; he wondered about the gun again; and suddenly he remembered that they hadn't had breakfast.

Zero came.

"Driver advance."

Everything was blotted out except the few yards of grass and bushes in front of the tank, the place where he had to pass through the infantry. As the tank moved forward, he saw helmets where men crouched low in a trench, waiting for the order to get up and walk upright. Then there was just the pressure of his brow on the periscope pad, and ahead an open flatness, ending in a line of flickering explosions.

115

He tried to see which of the explosions was the gun; but it might have been any one of them. The shots went slamming through the air. It was still more than three-quarters dark.

"Hello, Oboe three . . ."

A Lancer troop moved up on his left, their Besas spitting tracer. They were going to shoot him in. He felt an intense comradeship with the long Cromwells. They and he were out ahead—the little black arrows on the war maps.

"Co-ax, five hundred, fire!"

His own gunner opened up, and the fumes blew back into the turret, sharp and choking, towards the ventilator fan.

"Just keep spraying, gunner."

They moved with infinite slowness. It seemed to be getting lighter, but really it was just the distance closing. The low black line of the trees emerged; the spire of the church, dim against the dawn.

"Get ready, flame-gunner—fire!"

The flame shot out, fell, broke, rolled along the ground.

"Left, sir. Left!"

Suddenly, from the side of the periscope, Wilson saw something flash against the armour of a Cromwell. The driver jerked the Crocodile towards a small, dark opening in the trees, and for one long moment the flame-gunner pumped in the fire.

They worked down the trees which masked the front of the village, pouring the fire into the darkness. Now and again there was the sound like men screaming, which Wilson had once heard in Normandy. When they reached the end of the trees, Wilson halted the troop and they stood off the target while the infantry went in.

Two minutes later Barber came on the air. "Our friends are held up," he said. "Go in and help them."

He led the Crocodiles into another opening in the trees, and everything went dark again. The front of his tank began to nose up a tall bank; it lifted slowly, reached the top and stood poised for a moment. All at once the bank gave way.

"She's slipping," shouted the driver. "I can't hold her."

One of the tracks started to race. The tank began to turn over, sliding a little, rolling on its side. Wilson thought: We shall be helpless, like an upside-down turtle. Next moment the tank slid off the bank and crashed into a dark space below.

His head must have struck the gun mechanism. When he came to, the tank was on its side. The seventy-five and the Besa were useless. The wireless was dead. All he could see was the red indicator lamp of the flame gun, which still glowed on the turret wall.

"Are you all right in front?"

The flame gunner answered, sounding dazed.

"Can you see anything?"

"Yes, a house."

"All right, flame it."

The flame shot out. Its sudden glow lit up the periscopes. He leant against the seventy-five ejector shield and tried to manipulate them, straining to see the enemy who must be coming in with their Bazookas. But the periscopes would move only a few degrees.

He directed the flame to the only other target he could find—a group of cottages, a little to the right, about a hundred yards away. The fire crashed in and ran through the buildings from end to end. It's always the same, he thought. Flame anything in sight and you're terrifying. Stop, and you're a sitting target for the Bazookas. But, fired continuously, the flame lasted only a few minutes.

All at once, the gun gave the snort which meant that the fuel tanks were empty.

"Take your guns and get out," he said.

They climbed out with their Sten guns, and made a small group round the Crocodile. He saw now that, coming over the bank, it had run onto the roof of a small house. The house had collapsed and the tank had fallen down among the rubble. The battle was going on all around.

"Wait here," he said. "I'll try to find the others."

He took a Sten and went through some bushes to the left, where there was firing. A few moments later he found himself in a sunken garden: it must have been the garden of the place they called the Rectory. There was an ornamental summerhouse in the middle, and a gate in the wall on the far side.

It seemed quite empty. Then he saw the German officer. He was standing ten yards away, with a pistol in his hand; and he saw Wilson at the same moment.

Wilson pressed the trigger of his Sten. He thought: It's the first time I've killed a man this way. But nothing happened. He tugged at the cocking handle. The Sten was jammed.

Slowly the German raised his pistol and fired. The bullets smacked dully into the bushes at Wilson's back. It seemed so stupid. He was struggling to get out his own pistol, which was caught in the lining of his pocket.

Then the German turned and ran. As he went through the gate, a Bren gun fired on the far side of the wall: he tilted sideways and fell in a little heap.

Wilson found the Bren and a corporal in charge of it.

"Have you seen the Crocodiles?"

"Frig, no," said the corporal. "But the place is lousy with Jerries." He was going in to clear the Rectory. His

118

men were all-out. They'd been doubling in through the
Spandau fire, and now he was urging them on again.

At last he got them to their feet. They ran across a lawn
and the corporal threw a grenade through the door. As they
went in, he shot left and right through every door with the
big German Schmeiser he was carrying.

Wilson watched them, and then went off through the
trees again, hoping to pick up track-marks or perhaps find
Barber. At the foot of a big oak a German lay clutching his
stomach. He was half moaning, half shrieking. As Wilson
passed, the noise subsided to a sob, and he saw that the man
was dying.

Beyond was a kind of garden shed, ripped open by a
shell and full of smashed bicycles. There must have been
twenty or thirty—tall Dutch bicycles, with pieces of German
equipment tied to them. Then there was a trench with a
pile of bodies. When Wilson crossed, he found the open
ground.

He was facing the knocked-out Cromwell. The crew had
tried to bale out. One, a boy of about nineteen, was lying
on the ground with his head on his arm; he was smiling,
as if asleep, and his brain had spilled out on his battledress.

Further on, Barber's Support tank was trying to pull a
Crocodile out of the stream. Wilson ran over.

"What's happened?" said Barber.

Wilson told him. "Who's tank is this?" he asked.

"One of Sherrif's."

"Let me have it."

Just then the Support tank pulled the Crocodile free.
The corporal tank commander handed over the headset,
and Wilson took the Crocodile into the village.

He found the rest of the troop and told them to follow
him. At the end of the village six or seven Cromwells were

firing across the fields. He led the troop into position among some broken buildings.

The ground ahead was utterly flat, except for a single hedge, and away in the distance a row of haystacks. For a moment it was difficult to see what the Cromwells were firing at. Then, unexpectedly, the early morning sun broke through a cloud bank, lighting up the ground in clear detail.

Wilson ran his glasses over the pattern of greens and browns, which a moment before had been monochrome. Almost at once his eye caught something moving—a line of grey figures which doubled and paused and doubled again, moving across the front, left to right, towards the 'sHertogenbosch road.

"Co-ax. traverse right. Steady . . . on. Six hundred. Got them, gunner?"

The gunner spun his elevating wheel.

"On, sir."

"Fire!"

The Besa broke into a roar, hosing out tracer in a flat arc. The burst fell short but quickly moved up, cutting into the figures as they ran. Through his glasses Wilson saw some stumble and fall. The rest went to ground.

Then another group was running.

"Co-ax. stop. Up two hundred, left."

The gun began to hose them. Quickly the sergeant and corporal picked up the target. But the group went on, a man or two dropping at a time. Wilson saw now that they were making for one of the haystacks. Suddenly he remembered what the sergeant-major had said.

"Co-ax. stop. Seventy-five load A.P."

The operator opened the breech, ejected the high-explosive round which lay there, and threw in the long black armour-piercing shot.

"Seventy-five traverse right."

The turret swung right with a gentle whine from the traverse motor.

"Steady . . . on. Haystack eight hundred. Fire!"

There was the usual convulsion as the gun fired; the breech running back on recoil; a haze of flame and heat above the muzzle; the shot with its single red trace, spinning towards the target.

As it struck, there was a violent flash. The haystack burst into flame and poured out smoke—the thick black smoke which comes from fuel oil.

The operator threw in another round.

Suddenly the Lancers were firing A.P. too. Then, without warning, something big and square emerged from a haystack further along the line. It moved sedately from left to right, gradually gathering speed. Wilson brought over his gun, and twice the gunner fired at it. But it was no good. The thing disappeared in a sunken road.

He wirelessed back to the Lancers squadron commander, who was at the other end of the village.

"Hello Item Two, there's a Tiger just gone across our front, moving your way. Over."

"Hello, Item Two. Thanks for the tip. Out."

For the first time Wilson felt sure of himself in battle. More than that, he was elated. He'd led in the infantry, flamed an anti-tank gun, burned down half a dozen buildings which might or might not have held enemy, switched tanks, knocked out what was generally thought to have been a Mark IV in a haystack, and seen a Tiger long enough to fire at it.

"Well," said Barber. "Did you have a good time?"

"Fine," said Wilson.

The squadron was going back to refuel, and he went off to find his own crew. When he reached them, the fitters had arrived with the A.R.V. and were fixing tow-ropes to pull the Crocodile upright. The place was full of smoke from the burned cottages. Every now and then a mortar bomb fell, and they all dived under the A.R.V. for shelter.

Presently the mortaring slackened, and they made breakfast. There was a tin of bacon and some jam and biscuits. They ate happily and almost silently in a place where they could see no dead, knowing that the Crocodile would be out of action for a good many hours yet.

When they had finished, the gunner disappeared in the direction of the Rectory. A few minutes later he came back with a handful of black cigars.

"Have one, sir. They're out of a Jerry funk hole."

But Wilson shook his head. He pulled a crumpled Player's from his pocket and stood for a moment, listening to the sound of firing, which now came from far on the other side of the village.

"I'm going for a walk. If you want me, I'm up where the anti-tank gun was."

Ever since his first action in Normandy he'd been drawn by a fierce curiosity to see what happened where they'd flamed. Yet he'd never done so, because always they'd be switched from one place to another, and there was never a chance to explore the objective.

He walked down the front of the trees, where here and there the brushwood still smouldered among the blackened trunks. The burning away of the undergrowth had completely uncovered some trenches. He looked in the first and for the moment saw only a mass of charred fluff. He wondered what it was, until he remembered that the Germans were always lining their sleeping-places with looted bedding.

A " Flail " in action.

AVRE going forward with a fascine.

Crocodiles flaming a farm-house.

Cross-channel gun at Cap Gris Nez.

Then, as he was turning to go, he saw the arm. At first he thought it was the charred and shrivelled crook of a tree root; but when he looked closer, he made out the hump of the body it was attached to. A little way away was the shrivelled remains of a boot.

He went on to the next trench, and in that there was no concealing fluff. There were bodies which seemed to have been blown back by the force of the flame and lay in naked, blackened heaps. Others were caught in twisted poses, as if the flame had frozen them. Their clothes had burned away. Only their helmets and boots remained, ridiculous and horrible.

He wanted to vomit. He'd vomited before at some sights. But now he couldn't.

Suddenly he heard someone behind him and he looked round with a start. It was Randall, his flame-gunner. He must have come round from the opposite direction.

One didn't make favourites in a crew, but from the moment he'd taken over, Wilson had felt a special affection for Randall. With his constant cheekiness, his eternal arguments with the turret crew, he was utterly free from all false sentiment. He was a soldier because he had to be. He took no pride in killing.

"Come up and see what's by the gun," said Randall.

They went. The gun itself was crushed. One of the Cromwells or one of the other Crocodiles had run over it. A little to the side were the bodies of the crew. One of them had been caught by the flame as he ran away, splashed with the liquid which couldn't be shaken off. His helmet had fallen off and now he lay with black eyeballs, naked and charred and obscene.

There came from it all an enormous disgust, which couldn't be expressed, yet somehow one had to say something.

"We certainly did a proper job of it," said Randall.

About midday they had the Crocodile upright and joined the broken tracks. It was a makeshift job, because they had to break off some steel keepers which held the track pins in place.

On the way back to the refuelling point they met the rest of the squadron coming out.

"Catch us up when you're ready," shouted Barber.

As the column passed, Wilson saw his sergeant—Warner. Barber had put him with Sherrif's troop to replace a corporal who'd been killed in the village. Warner waved as he went by.

A little further on they had to let a scout car pass. As the car came level, it stopped, and the man in the commander's seat dismounted. It was Waddell.

He asked Wilson how the action had gone and where the squadron was. Wilson told him. The C.O. looked at the Crocodile, scored with bullets and with all its track guards ripped away, and grinned.

"Fine," he said, and then with a curious finality: "Good luck." Next moment the scout car disappeared towards the squadron in a cloud of dust.

The refuelling-field was littered with piles of empty drums. Wilson took the Crocodile round the perimeter until he found his own drums, full and neatly stacked, together with five new nitrogen cylinders.

They started heaving the heavy drums to the top of the trailer and pouring in the four hundred gallons of white, treackly flame-fuel. While they were doing it, the fitter sergeant arrived.

"You're not taking her out again without those keepers fixed?" he said.

"They'll hold a bit longer."

Sergeant Pye shook his head. "I'll go back and get the welding kit."

"Too long," said Wilson. "There's a R.E.M.E. section down the road. Go and borrow theirs."

Pye went off in his half-track.

"What did you do that for?" said Randall. "We could have been here till tomorrow."

Wilson didn't answer. Even if he had wished to answer, he couldn't have explained what the sight of those bodies at Rosmalen meant—that either one threw up everything and made one's protest, as William Home had, or else one did everything more thoroughly and conscientiously than ever before, so that there was no time to think.

Beyond Rosmalen the road went over a railway and into a waste of long, geometrical polder. Everything had become very quiet. To judge from the messages which came across the net, the squadron was three or four miles further on. They were moving with the infantry towards a place called Hintham.

The road was empty, except for returning ambulances and once, surprisingly, a Y.M.C.A. canteen van, whose driver had stopped at a cross-roads and was earnestly looking at his map.

The Crocodile passed the remains of some cottages. They must have been caught in the five-five bombardment. There were only the foundations left, with here and there some household possession—a bed or a stove—sticking out of the embers. Standing in front were the families who had lived in them. As the tank went by, they waved and cheered.

Soon afterwards there was a small village. From the talk on the wireless, Wilson knew that he must be right on the tail of the squadron now. There was a fork in the road.

"Which way do I go?" said the driver.

"Right," said Wilson. "Follow the track marks."

The driver changed down. The tank nosed up a narrow lane between two bungalows. A moment later they were among some empty chicken runs and vegetable plots at the back. Fields stretched beyond, ending in a line of poplars.

There was no sign of the squadron.

"Halt," said Wilson.

They halted. He was just pressing the switch of his microphone to call Barber, when the driver spoke suddenly over the intercom.

"I say, sir. Just have a look. These aren't British track marks. They're too wide."

It all happened very quickly then. There was the slam of a shot across the front of the tank. It was impossible to tell where it came from. He shouted "Make for cover", and the driver crashed the tank into a plot full of runner-beans and wire-netting.

"Driver, halt!"

Among the beans, he swung the cupola, trying to find the enemy.

Immediately there were four or five shots in succession. This time they came unmistakably from the left, where the other fork of the road ran. Suddenly he saw the whole situation. The squadron had taken that fork. Now at that moment it was running into an ambush.

Before he could do anything, the whole place came alive with the crash of mortars and machine-guns and anti-tank guns. Confused and frantic calls flew over the wireless, sometimes jamming each other. From a group of bungalows, two S.P.s were firing at fifty yards' range. Barber was trying to get the Crocodiles off the narrow road; the Lancers were trying to rush up a pair of heavy-gunned Shermans.

All the time someone kept calling to Barber: "Hello, Item, one of your babies has been hit."

Then at last there was a crash, which sounded like the Sherman seventeen-pounders in action. Under cover of their guns, Barber was ordering the Crocodiles to pull out.

Wilson manœuvred back to the road fork. As he reached it, there was a loud clatter, and Sherrif's troop came swinging by. There were only two tanks. Sherrif and his operator were leaning out of their hatches, clutching two troopers who lay slumped across the turret bin.

They were Warner's driver and co-driver.

Warner had been killed—good, brave, irreplaceable Warner, whose letters home he had censored week by week. With him died his gunner. They couldn't have known anything about it. An S.P. got them at fifteen yards' range through the back of the turret.

IX

'sHERTOGENBOSCH SHUTTLE-SERVICE

AFTER the ambush, while the squadron waited on the road into 'sHertogenbosch, Wilson asked Barber why Waddell had come round. Barber told him that Waddell had come to say goodbye. So Wilson learned the last chapter of the episode of William Douglas Home.

It had always seemed to him that Waddell, more than anyone else, had refused to accept the sincerity of William's protests. Or, if he had accepted it, he had never believed that in the last extremity William would defy the vast machinery of military discipline.

When William refused to obey the order to go into action at Le Havre, Waddell had been so disgusted or nonplussed that he delayed for several days before putting him under arrest. For this failure to observe the rules of discipline, the Divisional Commander had relieved him of command of the regiment.

When Wilson knew, he went back to his tank to think over what had happened.

Throughout every major action the Crocodiles had done, Waddell had been at work behind the scenes, planning the battle, exercising his influence on formation commanders, guarding the machine he'd created from misuse. The regiment was his handiwork. What would become of it in the future?

It took two days to get into 'sHertogenbosch. A troop would be sent forward to flame something, and as it came

128

back for more fuel it would pass another pressuring up for the next target. On the afternoon of the second day Wilson's troop was waiting by the roadside. A little way ahead was a column of big six-wheeled trucks piled high with pontoons and bridging equipment. The drivers were talking with civilians, who had the habit of appearing from nowhere immediately the battle had rolled over them.

"I wouldn't mind swopping places with those cushy bastards," said Randall.

As he spoke, Barber came through on the wireless: "Hello, Fox Four, go forward. . . ."

Today it was Fox; yesterday it had been Mike, the day before that Item. The code letter was changed for security.

Wilson switched to the intercom and told the driver to start up.

They rolled into the town with its noise of battle and over-hanging cloud of grey smoke. The sun had come out and the place was full of the smells of hot weather—petrol and street dust. Every now and then there was a heavy explosion as the Germans blew another bridge.

They passed the wreck of a field-gun with mangled horses in the traces, and suddenly there was a fresh look of death about it all. A little further on there was firing, and an infantry major was waiting. Wilson got down and ran over to him.

"When can you be ready?" said the major.

"Five minutes."

He showed Wilson the map and explained what was happening.

The enemy had been driven back across a canal and was making a new defence line on the far side of it. A troop of Lancers was going up a nearby street to try and seize an un-blown bridge. If they failed, the Crocodiles would support the infantry over the only remaining crossing—a little weir, which was likely to be under heavy fire.

While the Company Commander was speaking, there was an outburst of firing and a dull thud. A few minutes later a runner arrived to say that one of the Lancers' tanks had been Bazooka'd. It was beginning to brew up, and from across the block you could hear the ammunition exploding.

"Well," said the Company Commander, "it's all yours now."

Wilson ran back and told the crews to pressure up.

They slammed the trailers shut and pulled down the turret hatches. The infantry were waiting to follow them, huddled in doorways, trying to keep clear of mortars.

"Driver, advance."

The Crocodile jerked forward and next moment it was swinging round a corner. There was a rubble-filled street, and down at the end, a couple of hundred yards away, a building which must be beyond the water. It was a very narrow street, with no room to turn, and looking back to see that his sergeant's and corporal's tanks were following, Wilson felt a sudden claustrophobia.

Once, twice, dark narrow alleys gave on to the street from the side. He waited for the Bazooka out of the shadows; but it didn't come—and then they were approaching the blank face of the building on the far bank.

"Flame," shouted Wilson.

The flame leapt out across the water and splashed on the face of the building. It was wooden; the end of a terrace of dwelling-houses. The weir was just in front of it, festooned with coils of barbed wire.

"Long bursts, left and right!"

Just then something exploded on the roadway a few feet in front of the tank. An infantry corporal dashed forward with a pair of wire-cutters in his hand. Bullets cut the flagstones, throwing off sparks. The corporal fell, still grasping the cutters.

The Spandaus kept firing. You couldn't locate them. You knew only that they were in the houses on the far bank. Wilson got up his sergeant's and corporal's tanks into a little space on either side of him, and together they pumped in the flame methodically, left and right, as far as the guns could reach.

Presently there was no need to go on.

The infantry ran out again, sheltering themselves not from bullets now but from sparks and heat, and cut at the wire. In a minute or so they were pouring across the narrow cat-walk above the sluice gates.

Barber called the troop to go back and refuel, and Wilson started to reverse down the street. Suddenly, to his amazement, he found it blocked by a staff car. There was some apparatus inside and a figure with a war correspondent's tabs on his battle-dress.

The figure leant out and looked up.

"Excuse me, old man, but you couldn't do a bit more of that, could you? The bloody recording machine broke down . . ."

They came back past the carcasses of the German gun horses, already stripped bare of meat by the Dutch, and early next day the squadron crossed the canal by a Bailey bridge. They found themselves on a triangular island about three square miles in area. The enemy held half of it.

They drove into a little ornamental park, full of pampas grass and fishponds, and waited for the infantry to call them into action. Five minutes later the enemy started shelling. To the tank crews the shelling meant little. They stayed

131

beneath closed hatches and listened as the shells crashed round them. No damage was done, except that now and then the wireless would go dead and someone would have to open up the hatches and stick a new aerial in the socket.

For the infantry reserve company, who were dug in around them, it was tragically different. Every five minutes a shell would hit one of their slit-trenches. Men would lie moaning while the stretcher-bearers were called up, and then there would be a flurry of activity to get them away before the next salvo fell.

After a time the reserve company was pulled back, but runners kept crossing the park on their way to the forward companies. It became almost unendurable to watch them. You wondered if they knew that the 105s struck so swiftly. Many of them walked almost carelessly. One man fell a few yards in front of Wilson's tank. Wilson got out and dragged him into cover beneath it, and a moment later another shell exploded, leaving a little cloud of dust and smoke in the place where he'd been lying.

The squadron stayed there all day.

About four o'clock the shelling ceased for a while. There was fighting a couple of streets away, but civilians began to appear. They came up to the tanks. The crews tried to make them take cover, but they took no notice. Before anyone knew what was happening, others came from the broken houses at the edge of the park, bringing cups of ersatz coffee. They continued to bring coffee even after the shelling recommenced.

Then, towards evening, there was a loud noise of machine-guns. A call came over the net. A troop of Lancers rolled by, the troop leader with his flaps still open and his head bent over his microphone. They disappeared into the smoke, which was gradually drifting over all the park from burning buildings.

Wilson waited.

A few minutes later there was the muffled slam of a high-velocity gun.

A jeep appeared, bouncing between clumps of pampas. The driver shouted up:

"Fourteen Troop, Crocodiles?"

"Yes."

"You're wanted up ahead, sir."

Wilson jumped down. As he climbed into the jeep a salvo fell, throwing clods of earth all around. The driver raced the jeep forward, skidding the wheels. Next moment they were running through banks of smoke.

Beyond the park a big municipal-looking building was alight on its top floor. Bits of masonry were falling, adding to the rubble in the roadway. Then the jeep swung round a bend, and there was a single Lancer tank pulled into the side of the road. A white-faced corporal stared blankly from his open hatch, heedless of the mortar bombs which had started to fall.

There was no sign of the troop leader. A second tank was fifty yards beyond, apparently on a corner. It was burning like a blow-torch, the flames roaring out of the turret. As they came near it a batch of ammunition exploded, blowing out a tall plume of sparks.

"Better come quickly," said the jeep driver.

They jumped out and ran through the heat into a big building of concrete, which turned out to be a garage. The infantry C.O. was waiting with a group of his officers.

"All here now?"

"Yes," said someone, and they went up a ramp to the first storey.

There was a big window in the wall. They all stood back from it and looked through on to the next street. There was supposed to be a Tiger there. Wilson couldn't see it. Then one of the infantry officers lent him a pair of glasses, and about a hundred yards away he saw a square plate of yellow among some rubble.

All the time the C.O. had been talking with one of his company commanders. Wilson had only a vague idea what they were discussing, but it had something to do with the Crocodiles driving round the corner and flaming the Tiger as they came up the street. It seemed so remote, so fantastic a plan, that he couldn't believe it. It was part of a nightmare.

The C.O. turned to him. He was about to speak.

But just at that moment Barber arrived. Crocodiles were scarce—there were only fifty in the whole of the Allied command—and Barber had authority to stop them being used suicidally. As soon as he heard the plan, he rejected it. There was a little more talk, and they went back to the park on foot. The municipal building was now blazing brightly in the dusk. An infantryman told them to double because of snipers.

That night the infantry got the Tiger with a PIAT anti-tank grenade.

Battle was mostly a series of unheroic things—little successes, little escapes, long periods of waiting. Today, you could say to yourself, I went up a street and flamed some houses. Or, today we got away with it—no one called us in. It just went on from day to day, and it was enough that you were still there.

It took nearly a week to get the whole of 'sHertogenbosch. For the squadron it was all a matter of running down narrow streets, hoping for the best as one crossed intersections.

By the third or fourth day they thought that all the enemy's armour had been spotted—the Tiger and the Mark IV up by the railway station, the two S.P. guns across the second canal, and so on. But they were wrong.

It was Sherrif's turn to go in—another action near the concrete garage. Over the wireless Wilson heard Sherrif order his troop to advance. He followed his progress on the map, imagined him swinging his periscope as he came to a certain side-turning. Then suddenly Sherrif was shouting to his sergeant about something on the right. There was the slam of a gun in the headphones—and then silence. It was all so familiar now; you waited with a feeling of sickness to know who'd come up on the air again, and who wouldn't.

Presently the sergeant came up. There was a lot of confusion. Sherrif had been hit, but his tank was still running and the troop had flamed the target.

Barber kept calling, but minutes passed and Sherrif didn't reply. Then all at once there was a loud rattle, and the troop appeared down the street.

Sherrif's flaps opened. A moment later Sherrif himself appeared. He looked rather scared. There was a big hole in the turret. A shot had gone through the front armour and buried itself in the side wall. You could see the tail of the shot, melted and fused with the armour, about six inches inside.

That evening Duffy came up from the infantry division headquarters and told them he'd got a new harbouring area for the squadron. He was good at that kind of thing. It was just what was wanted—an undamaged street of small houses, just outside the enemy's mortar range. But when they came in, everyone was tired and on edge.

One of Wilson's drivers knocked down the little brick wall in front of one of the gardens. Duffy made a scene about it. Although the driver kept silent, he was in a fury; and when Duffy had gone, he started cursing him. Wilson told the driver to shut up. But the business angered and irritated him. The driver couldn't help what he had done.

The house which was given to Wilson's crew was full of cheap furniture, ugly and uncomfortable but lovingly preserved. He shone his torch on the box-like easy-chairs, the varnished coffee-table and the bookcase with its gilt-lettered encyclopaedia. It was an utterly civilian house, normal and remote from the war.

He went into the kitchen, looking for water for the tea dixie. There was a gleaming enamelled stove, saucepans and casseroles, white plates in a rack. Then he turned on the tap. It swivelled in his hand, squeakily, as dry taps do. And the illusion of normality ended.

After a meal the crews spread out their blankets on the floor. Wilson slept in a cubby-hole beneath the stairs with his head against the wall, which shook all night from the firing of a battery of twenty-five pounders in some nearby fields. It was a comforting sound. Whenever he woke up, he listened to it sensuously, thinking how good it was to be out of the battle for the moment.

On the last morning of the 'sHertogenbosch battle a bridge was to be laid to take the squadron across the final canal. The enemy seemed to be shooting off all his remaining ammunition. As the Crocodiles rumbled through the streets to the forward area, mortar bombs and shells were continually landing on the roofs of houses and showering the streets with tiles.

They came into a square. A shell had hit one of the big pontoon-carrying lorries, and it was blazing from end to end with great circles of flaring rubber where the tyres had been.

136

A little beyond—a block away from no-man's land—Dutch firemen with curious helmets and an antique engine were trying to save the contents of a grocer's shop.

They came to the canal-side. The infantry had crossed an hour or so before in assault boats, and now the bridge was being placed in position by a bridge-laying tank. It carried the bridge in place of a turret. As it approached the canal it lifted it up on a big hydraulic arm, balanced it high in the air for a moment, then gently lowered it, till the span dropped into place across the water.

The tank withdrew, and the squadron crossed.

Beyond the canal the town had the hostile atmosphere of newly taken ground. It was an area of workshops and railway yards, and Barber told Wilson to pull in his troop in a street of dilapidated workmen's houses. There was sporadic mortaring and shelling, and now and again some machine-gun fire.

About three in the afternoon an infantry company captain asked Wilson to come and look at some ground. They went between factory sheds and crossed the main railway track. To the right was the beginning of the town station. The Tiger there had been knocked out by the Lancers, but there was still shooting among derelict wagons on the sidings.

Beyond the railway they dropped into an abandoned enemy trench. This was the town's furthermost edge. Ahead it was all open country, flat and featureless, except for a distant line of poplars, and over to the left—about 800 yards away—a group of red buildings, which the map said were barracks. There was nothing moving there. A faint haze lay over the country.

They were going to take the barracks and the main worry was some S.P.s and 105s, which were supposed to be out in the polder a mile or so away. The captain explained the

137

battalion plan. The Crocodiles would go in first, covered by a troop of assault guns. Zero was at 1800 hours.

The scheme of attack looked dangerously easy. While the crews waited uneasily they made tea on the petrol stoves set up inside the tanks. Ten minutes before zero they pressured up and Wilson led them to the start-line.

There was no preparatory artillery shoot. At zero he merely gave the order to advance and they clattered across the railway, firing their Besas and driving line-abreast towards the barracks. There was some machine-gun and anti-tank-gun fire, but it was impossible to tell where it came from.

Halfway across the open ground, the Crocodiles slowed down to flame some trenches and a group of wooden huts. In the middle of flaming, the corporal's tank slid sideways into a half-finished anti-tank ditch and stuck there with its tail in the air. Wilson and his sergeant went on towards the objective. As they swung in among the tall, blank barrack-blocks, it was clear that the place itself was abandoned. The infantry came in, and he heard them going through the buildings, firing now and then or throwing a grenade. No one returned the fire, but the Crocodiles had to wait there till they got their release.

For some reason the release took a long time. When it came over the wireless, it was already nightfall. The infantry had disappeared. No one knew if they had gone on, or withdrawn into the town. Suddenly the whole situation seemed uneasy and sinister.

Wilson drove to the corporal's tank and fixed a tow-rope. But just as he had pulled the corporal's tank out of the ditch, his own fell into another ditch concealed in the darkness. This time there was no getting out without a proper towing-tank.

He picked up the microphone to call Barber.

At that moment there was a sudden roar and shudder. It stunned him for a second. When he looked through the periscopes, the ground all around was erupting with shell bursts. They felt like 105s and they were coming in without warning.

He wondered why it happened only now. Then he realised that in the falling darkness the Crocodiles were lit up by the fire from the wooden huts, which still blazed brightly about a hundred yards away.

He pressed the "send" switch of the microphone.

"Hello Sugar Two, report my signals. Over."

But the only answer was a violent whine. It had come through quite often in the past few days. The net was being jammed.

There was no point in keeping the sergeant and corporal. He told them to take their tanks back to harbour and send up the towing tank.

As time dragged on the shelling settled down to salvoes every thirty seconds. It was quite beyond anything they had known in the park. A terrific crack on the turret put out the roof lamps. He saw the operator looking at him in the red light of the indicator lamp on the wireless. There were fragments of glass on his shoulder from a smashed periscope.

A little later there were two direct hits on the trailer. It was much less heavily armoured than the tank and he wondered how much it would stand. There were three hundred gallons of unspent flame-fuel inside. Other shells struck and he knew that all the fittings on the outside of the tank were going—the bin where they stored their bedding, the remaining track-guards, the track-plates welded to the armour to stop bazookas.

After forty minutes there was a pause. He opened the flaps to put up a new wireless aerial. There was a curious silence outside. The fire of the huts had died down, and there were only the glowing embers. Somewhere quite close a machine-gun fired.

Another half-hour.

"Shall I try again?" said the operator. He had been calling at intervals, hoping he might get through the jamming. There had been no answer. Gradually Wilson had become convinced that the towing tank had come out and missed them.

The operator called:

"Hello, Sugar Two. . . ."

Suddenly there was a distorted reply. All they heard was the code-sign, but for the moment it was enough that out in the darkness someone of their own was looking for them.

Minute by minute the calls of the towing tank grew stronger, till at last it could be only a few hundred yards away. The shelling was coming in rushes again. A salvo, a gap of thirty seconds or a minute, and then the next one.

Presently Wilson saw the shape of a Churchill nosing across his front towards the embers of the huts. He got out of the tank and ran towards it. The Churchill changed direction. There was someone leading it on foot. It was Harding, the driver whom Duffy had slated for knocking down the wall.

"Get down," Wilson shouted.

The Churchill stopped, and they lay with their faces to the ground. The next shells struck, filling the night with noise and bitter smoke. Then the Churchill backed on to the Crocodile, and they hitched up the towing-cable.

All the while as they were screwing up the shackles, waiting for the next salvo to end everything, Harding swore genially in cockney.

At last it was done. The towing tank took the strain, there was a jerk on the cable and the Crocodile ground its way out of the ditch.

As they crawled back to the railway, Wilson looked round at the explosions of succeeding salvoes. The enemy seemed unaware that they had left.

X

THE MEIJEL ROAD

IN October, 1944, there was still an idea that the Second Army would be into Germany by the winter. A few days after 'sHertogenbosch, Sherrif's troop was detached for some mysterious exercise. It was taking place to the south, well behind the front-line.

After a short rest the remainder of the squadron was sent down too. They harboured in a little village and the first night, as soon as it was dark, they drove out in trucks to see what Sherrif was doing.

The ground had been selected, although they didn't know it then, because it resembled a sector on the German border. There were even some dummy trenches and dugouts. Sherrif's troop was pressuring up. A company of infantry was deployed behind them, and several hundred yards away, on slightly higher ground, stood a section of searchlights. You couldn't see the searchlights, but you knew they were there because of the throbbing of the generator motors.

Sherrif came over and—with an obvious lack of conviction—explained what was supposed to happen. Then he went back and mounted his Crocodile.

A few moments later the troop began to advance. Simultaneously the searchlights were switched on, and the ground ahead was bathed in hard, blue light. There was a little spurt of flame as the flame-gunners tested ignition, then they started flaming. They ran through their carpet of fire, shooting the fuel into the trenches, till they came to the end of the run. Then the infantry swept through them, uttering wild cries like a crowd in school Shakespeare.

"Now they'll do it again," said an infantry officer.

For the next run the spectators were told to stand behind the trenches. They were asked to imagine themselves in the place of the enemy, harassed by shell-fire, blinded by the searchlights, suddenly confronted with a squadron of flame throwers.

Wilson stood with the rest and imagined. But his imagination took all the wrong directions. He wasn't a harassed infantryman, but a German anti-tank gunner. And he wasn't blinded. As soon as the searchlights went on, he wondered why the Tommies were so obligingly silhouetting all these big slow-moving targets. When the targets turned out to be flame throwers, it was easier still. Between shots, the flame-guns were never quite extinguished; they continued to drip with a little beard of fuel, which burned and flared on the tanks' front armour. They might as well be driving with their road-lamps on.

A few nights later they brought out the rest of the Crocodiles and did the assault as a squadron. The commander of an infantry division was watching, and the flames and searchlights were lighting up the ground for miles around. When it was over, he came and addressed the troop leaders.

"Gentlemen," he said. "You and I are going to crack the Siegfried Line."

But Wilson, for one, was listening with only half an ear. The other half followed the noise of an aircraft, which was circling overhead in the darkness. Before the general could finish there was a sudden burst of power from the aircraft's engine, and a bomb exploded with a resounding crack in the next field.

They packed up earlier than usual.

No more was heard of the Siegfried Line project. But a few days later Duffy came into the drab little restaurant which served as a mess and said: "Wilson, you're going down to Helmond first thing tomorrow. The Germans are trying to cut the salient. They've got within nine miles of Army headquarters."

The road to Helmond was littered with burned-out British transport. At one point there were the remains of twenty or thirty R.A.S.C. three-tonners. Out in a field was the wreck of a German Mark IV. But the German tank commander, with all these fine, soft targets in his gun-sights, had stayed too long. A PIAT had got him.

Barber had gone ahead to contact an infantry division, but by the time the troop arrived the enemy had been stopped and thrown back a little. Two days later the whole squadron was assembled in the east of the salient, where a desultory battle had started in an attempt to push the enemy back further.

There was going to be an attack on a place called Meijel. It was to be mainly a tank attack, and the orders were given by a tank battalion colonel. He began by holding up the map. The Battalion was working with an infantry battalion on a one-mile front. What wasn't marsh on this front was minefield, and right on the line of advance was a sinister-looking wood. You had only to be told that there were three or four known eighty-eights in the wood to foresee the kind of mess there would be.

The colonel, undaunted, developed the plan of attack. The outstanding feature was Phase Two: one of the tank squadrons was going round the side of the wood to create a diversion. Wilson looked round the strange faces in the group, wondering which of the three majors commanded the lucky squadron—and if they'd give him his D.S.O. right now. But they were all bent over their maps, marking in the report lines for the later phases.

The Crocodiles were not being used till Phase Four, the assault on Meijel itself. They spent the night at a nearby village with a canal and a drawbridge straight out of Breughel. Early in the morning they moved out to the start-line and waited for zero.

The first part of the operation was simple. The whole force—tanks, Crocodiles and infantry—moved forward to a piece of high ground, which no one had occupied before because every square yard was ranged by the enemy's 105s. As soon as it was accomplished, Wilson waited for the diversion to begin.

It was a long wait, and all the time the 105s made the most of their opportunity. The Regiment's tanks stood nose to tail on a road. Wilson's troop was immediately behind them. Five minutes after they arrived, there was a direct hit on his trailer, and he saw that the armour had split.

Meanwhile the infantry were trying to dig in on the forward edge of the high ground, where the enemy could see every movement. Soon there was a regular procession of ambulance jeeps, racing back with loaded stretchers. It was the business of the ornamental park again: you watched with anxiety as they took their chances between salvoes.

Presently some drivers grew careless: the 105s were firing from a flank, and perhaps they thought that as long as they drove on the "sheltered" side of the tank column, everything was safe. It wasn't.

One driver, returning with empty stretchers, stopped level with Wilson's tank. He got out and began to urinate. A shell screamed down without warning. When the dust drifted off, the man lay dead. His jeep, unharmed, stood two yards away, puffing blue smoke from the exhaust pipe.

At last the squadron which was to make the "diversion" reported itself ready. There was a lot of calling on the wireless. Some twenty-five pounders gave a covering shoot. Besa fire came from the direction of the wood. The diversion had started.

For a minute the net went silent. Then a troop leader came on the air and reported that two of his tanks were bogged.

"Roger, Out," said the control station.

Wilson began to keep a tally. There were eighteen tanks in a squadron.

A moment later someone else came on the air. He'd gone on a mine. Then, when the squadron must have been almost level with the wood, the net was suddenly jammed by two or three stations together. When they had sorted themselves out it was found that the best part of three troops had gone on the minefield.

Control told the others to halt, and everyone waited for the inevitable.

It wasn't long coming.

At the first slam of an eighty-eight there was a frantic call for smoke. A tank troop ahead moved quickly up the road and deployed along the skyline.

Wilson shouted to his operator to load smoke in the seventy-five, the flat-nosed round went clanging into the breech and he calculated the elevation.

"Fire!"

The shell sailed slowly up, making a visible arc, and vanished towards the wood.

"Repeat."

He gave the elevation to the rest of the troop. It was all confusion now. The tanks of the regiment were firing from the ridge. From beyond came the slam of the anti-tank guns. On the minefield, crews of the "diversion" squadron were baling out and trying to get back to the infantry lines.

The smoke built up in a big white cloud. Then the firing of the eighty-eights changed its tone and direction. Wilson glanced towards the ridge and saw that one of the tanks there was burning: there was an ugly black cloud of petrol smoke and a little blaze of fire above the engine decks.

A moment later another caught fire, and the rest drew back a little.

Then the 105s struck. In all the confusion, Wilson had almost forgotten them. Suddenly there was a deafening crash and everything went red. In the strange silence which followed, Randall called through from the front compartment. The driver, Stone, had a periscope blown in on his face. They put him in an ambulance, and Randall took over the controls.

The shelling went on throughout the afternoon. Crews from the tanks on the minefield came doubling back like unhorsed jockeys. The infantry were trying to push on with Phase Three—the capture of a little village on the right flank. But they weren't making much progress.

The Crocodile crews made a meal of biscuits and corned beef, and the closed turrets grew warm and stale with tobacco smoke. Now and again one of the tanks would fire off its gun. The gesture had nothing to do with the battle; it was just that the Churchill made no provision for the wants of nature, and the only answer was to use a spent shell case.

Towards nightfall the Crocodiles withdrew. The battle was being re-planned, and they wouldn't be needed any longer.

There was central heating in the Town Hall at Zomeren, and it still worked. In a little café across the road there was a wood-stove, and there was fuel for that too. The officers slept in the Town Hall, and the crews in civilian billets. There was nothing more that anyone craved for.

After breakfast Wilson would walk across the frost-whitened field behind the billets and join his troop for maintenance. When they'd done the immediate tasks like tightening the tracks and changing oil, work eased off. They sat about talking and drinking the hot, sweet tea which the gunner brewed.

They talked about many things—cures for piles, God and atheism, the infrequency of the "D" Type Compo ration, and the charms of the girls in Zomeren. The only thing they didn't talk about was the next action.

Looking at his men, Wilson sometimes wondered what was his bond with them. It came to this: three months ago he'd taken them over as a stranger. They had known nothing about him and obeyed him only because they had to. Now they'd seen half a dozen battles together, and the troop had come through almost as a whole. They obeyed him because they trusted him.

Perhaps one might have thought it had something to do with leadership or skill. But Wilson knew well that it hadn't. It was luck.

In the evenings he would sometimes leave mess, which Duffy had set up in the café, and go over to the crews. The families they were billeted with were very hospitable. The first time he went, he found himself being led into a small family circle. The corporal introduced him to the old Dutch couple who presided.

"This is our officer," he said.

The old couple beamed and talked at him. When they had finished, the daughter explained in halting English: "They say you are very young for an officer."

On the sixth day in Zomeren Duffy arranged that liberty trucks should take the men into Eindhoven. They got out their Number One battle-dress, which had been travelling since they landed in the trucks of the rear echelon. Wilson and Sherrif paid them out and watched them go off, laughing and joking and teasing each other. Then they went and borrowed Duffy's jeep.

To drive into Eindhoven was to enter another world. There were cinemas showing the latest English and American films; a Naafi tea shop; shops with lighted windows; bars which glowed softly with their bottles of Geneva and Cherry Bols. Everyone knew that the squadron's time in rest was a short one. Tradition demanded that in such a situation a pair of young subalterns should get a little drunk. But curiously they did quite otherwise.

They went to a cinema and saw a Harry James film. There was a song with a recurrent line about "A young man with a horn." For anyone versed in British army slang, the phrase had a meaning which the American lyric-writer could scarcely have intended. They filled the auditorium with convulsive laughter, until they had to go out and recover.

In the evening they went to the Philips Radio Theatre and saw John Clements and Kay Hammond play *Blithe Spirit*. At the end there were eight or nine curtain calls, and when they came out, still with the inward glow of laughter, it was hard to believe that the wet cobbled street led up to the front again.

They were going out any day now. Wilson was in the turret, packing cigarettes into the box marked "Binoculars" on the turret wall, when his batman came up.

"Captain Barber would like to see you," he said.

Wilson went to the mess.

When he got there he found Dunkley there too.

"There's a job for you both," said Barber. "An infantry brigade wants you."

"With the vehicles?"

"No. By yourselves."

"What is it?"

"I don't know. You're supposed to take Sten guns."

The brigade was at Asten, about four miles away. Neither Wilson nor Dunkley spoke very much as they drove there in the scout car. It was a grey day, and they seemed to share a presentiment of something unpleasant.

They found brigade headquarters in a farmworker's house.

"Who are you from?" said the Staff Captain.

"Crocodiles," said Wilson.

"Oh yes," said the captain. "You've come to do the patrol." He gave them a map reference. "Go and see the battalion; they'll tell you all about it."

The map reference was in Meijel. The front had moved forward about two thousand yards since they were last there.

They drove down the road which the 105s had pounded. Meijel was badly smashed. As the scout car swung into the main street, mortaring started. An R.P. pointed to battalion headquarters and hurriedly directed the scout car between two buildings.

150

"We'd like you to look at the canal out there," said the infantry colonel. He was standing with his back to the sandbagged window, beyond which the mortar bombs were falling like rain-drops. "I suggest you go out as soon as it's dark. We'll give you an escort. See if you think you can flame across to the far bank."

He handed them over to the Adjutant, who showed them the situation map.

The canal was a mile to the east. The point where the infantry wanted to cross was enclosed by a semi-circle of trees a thousand yards forward from the nearest company.

"There might be some Germans on the near side—but not many," said the Adjutant.

After that he showed them the mines map. There were mines across the whole front, and in one place someone had written in the word "S-mines".

While they were talking, the mortaring had stopped. People were entering and leaving the building again.

"I expect you'd like to see what you can in daylight," said the Adjutant. He called a sergeant and told him to take them to the forward company.

The track from the village was marked with a tape strung out along bushes. Carriers had been along it and the ruts were full of water. In one place, where the bushes were all beaten down, there was a pile of spent eighty-eight cases. They must have been from the eighty-eight which picked off the tanks on the ridge.

Presently the track opened out and there was a group of slit trenches with camouflage capes thrown over them. Officers and soldiers were spooning cold stew from their mess tins. It was company headquarters.

A young lieutenant took over. He led them forward to a place where the bushes thinned out and a path went off to the left. "That's the way to our listening-post," he said. "This is as far as we can go in daylight."

Wilson and Dunkley looked out across a waste of meadows, and turned back.

At battalion headquarters the Adjutant met them.

"Happy?" he said.

Wilson nodded.

"Let's say you rendezvous here at seven o'clock then."

They had three hours to wait and they went back to Zomeren to get some warmer clothes. The crews were doing afternoon maintenance. The room in the Town Hall was empty. Wilson sat down on his bed and, fondly aware of the rough, familiar touch of the blankets, pulled on a sweater and thick socks.

When he was dressed, he went through his pockets, taking out anything which could identify the unit. There were a couple of letters from his mother. He stuffed them under his pillow and went down to the tanks to get some grenades.

"What the hell are they sending you to do?" said Randall.

Wilson told him.

"Frig that for a lark."

He dropped the grenades into his pocket and turned to go.

"Look after yourself," said Corporal Grossman.

"Good luck," said someone else. "We'll keep some char brewing."

He joined Dunkley, and feeling ridiculously theatrical with their weapons, they walked over to the mess to tell Barber they were off.

It had started to rain. They closed the roof of the scout car and huddled in the cramped seats, smoking a last cigarette.

"Where are we, driver?"

"Just gone through Asten, sir."

Wilson looked at his watch and tried to think how good it would be when they were riding back to the squadron in a couple of hours.

"We're coming into Meijel, sir."

The car slowed down, bouncing over potholes. They slid back the roof. Outside, in the dusk, there was distant firing.

"Pull up by the house on the left, driver."

Beside the house a little group was waiting. As Wilson dismounted, he made out the Adjutant. There was also an Armoured Corps sergeant who was coming to look at the ground for a Flail squadron, and a little man from the Royal Engineers.

"Fine," said the Adjutant. "The escort'll be here in a moment. You've got a good man going with you. An M.M. He's had plenty of experience with this kind of thing."

The Adjutant's promise was fulfilled. The sergeant was a big, rather casual man, and as soon as he spoke he imparted confidence. With him were a couple of privates with Sten guns, a lance-corporal, and another man with a Bren.

"Well," said the sergeant, "we might as well fix the details. We go out via the listening-post. There's a track leads out across the meadows there. When we get to the trees, we'll drop off the Bren to cover us out in case of trouble. After that I'll come forward with a couple of men to within about twenty yards of the bank. You won't want us barging about when you do the last bit."

He turned to the Adjutant.

"All right, sir?"

153

"All right," said the Adjutant. "Good luck."

They moved off in a ragged file down the taped path, the sergeant and the two Sten-gunners leading, the lance-corporal and the Bren-gunner at the rear.

There was a short delay when they reached the company position. Everyone talked in whispers. People kept calling the sergeant by his Christian name, and someone was sent to telephone the listening-post.

While they waited, Wilson took the Flails sergeant aside and they went through the procedure to be used on the canal bank. First Wilson and Dunkley would go up to a point on the right, and Wilson would look across. Then they'd move over to a point about fifty yards to the left, and Dunkley would do the looking. The sergeant would follow, but would stay at the bottom of the bank.

They formed up in file again. Suddenly Wilson noticed the little R.E. He was carrying an enormous rod.

"What about you? What are you supposed to do?"

It turned out that he had to measure the slope on the far side of the bank, to see if it was suitable for launching amphibious tanks.

In the end, it was fixed that he did his reconnaissance independently.

"All right," said the infantry sergeant. "No more talking."

They set off again, squelching through puddles. Presently the file changed direction. Wilson supposed they had passed the point where the track went off to the listening-post. He kept his eyes on the back of the man in front.

Suddenly there was a sharp whisper: "Halt, who goes there?"

The man in front stopped abruptly. You couldn't

Crocodiles in action at 'sHertogenbosch.

'sHertogenbosch: Across the canal.

Buffaloes crossing the Rhine

Infantry advancing under cover of flame (The Rhineland).

see anyone. A little way ahead the sergeant gave the password, and two figures emerged from a bush beside the path.

"All quiet?" said the sergeant.

There was a whispered conversation, and Wilson caught: "The boys are expecting you."

The file moved on. The outline of a building loomed up, solid against the dark sky. There were cobbles underfoot; it must be a barnyard.

They halted for a moment against a shed, and the sergeant went inside. There were muffled voices from beyond the thin wall. Someone cranked the handle of a field telephone. "They're leaving now," he said.

The moment they left the shelter of the farm buildings a wind caught them in gusts. They moved very slowly, five paces apart from each other. Every now and then the file would stop and they would freeze where they were, listening through the patter of the rain on the water-logged meadows.

There were four hundred yards to go. The blackness was everywhere, impenetrable and hostile. Wilson heard the loud squelch of water in one of his boots; and all the time he waited for a flare to go up, or the jabbing flame of a machine-gun.

Then he remembered the word "S-mines" on the map. At mines school they had taught him clever ways of finding S-mines: you crawled on your stomach with a twig in your hand to find the trip-wires. But tonight, in this darkened waste, the only way to find an S-mine was to tread on it.

Soon the file began to stop more frequently, and for much longer periods. He lost all sense of how far they'd come and how long they'd been out there. Then, from behind the British lines, a Bofors fired. The tracer soared above them—a pre-arranged direction signal. It was being fired half-hourly.

Presently they stood still for more than two minutes, and he knew they were inside the semi-circle of trees, because the wind was cut off.

There was a faint click—the lowering of the bipod legs of the Bren. The file began to move forward again, and the infantryman in front stepped sideways, sinking to the ground.

Wilson went forward, pausing at every other pace. A little way ahead a dark line of earth rose up. He wondered what would happen if he walked forward briskly and climbed it. Behind him he could hear Dunkley's breathing. He got down on his stomach and began to crawl.

As he approached the bank, he saw that it was too high to flame over—but if it were not too steep the Crocodiles might be able to nose half-way up. He started to climb, running his fingers through the wet grass for trip-wires and wondering where the enemy had his machine-guns. Then he felt a brush of wind above him and knew he was reaching the top.

He raised himself slowly. For a moment he thought he saw a German helmet, but it was only a bush which the wind was bending. He was fully up now, keeping his head near a clump of grass. It took almost a minute to distinguish between the solid form of the far bank and the liquid texture of the water which lapped it.

Then, as he was coming down, there was a little splash, like a lump of earth detaching itself a few yards up the bank.

The party crawled back a little, and made their way over

to the second point. They crawled through a ragged low hedge. There was the bank again, and Dunkley started to climb it. The air was very still. Somewhere far away an aircraft was droning through the rainclouds.

Suddenly there was an explosion—a flash which lit the bank with its tufts of grass and reeds.

Wilson looked round. There were flickering lights. Something stung his back. Mines, he thought—Dunkley's pulled a trip-wire.

Then he understood. Grenades.

Immediately there were explosions all around him. The stinging, curiously un-painful, curled round his body like the after-warmth of a school beating.

Fumbling in his pocket for his own grenades, he thought: where shall I throw them? I don't know where the enemy is. The pocket was warm and wet. He must have been hit.

He felt Dunkley beside him.

"Come on," said Dunkley. "Let's get out."

They got up and ran back to the hedge, grenades bursting behind them. When they reached the hedge, the infantry sergeant was waiting.

"Where are they?"

"Just the other side of the bank," said Dunkley.

"Better be off," said the sergeant.

But to Wilson it all seemed unreal. Suddenly he felt himself falling. Someone grabbed his arm.

"Are you hit?"

"Yes," he said, and then he remembered the Flails sergeant. He had been lying behind them, nearest to cover. Now he wasn't there.

"Christ," said Dunkley. "We've got to get him."

"Yes," said Wilson. Then he lost consciousness.

When he came to, there were more explosions. Dunkley and the infantry sergeant were coming through the hedge again. They hadn't been able to get near the Flails man.

"We're getting out," said Dunkley.

Wilson felt his elbows gripped and they were moving back home, across the meadows.

XI

ENGLISH FACES

TIME no longer counted. Life emerged as a series of sounds and smells. The smells were mostly iodine and ether, and the greatest sound was silence.

First, there was the silence of the regimental aid post. The doctor saying: "We've stopped the bleeding." The prick of a needle in his arm and the splash of rain on his face as they carried him outside. The luxurious silence of the ambulance as it padded over the road to the rear area.

Lying in the corridor of some hospital—and someone saying: "There must be a mistake, take him to the officers' ward." A few feet away was a young infantryman, grinning from his pillow: rather like Randall. He wanted to tell the orderly: "Let me stay here." But the tingling of the morphia intervened.

An aircraft—not a very modern one—bumping and swaying in an air current. His face was to the side of the fuselage, watching a control wire which moved to and fro. Then another ambulance. He was lifted off the stretcher and rolled onto a cold hard sheet.

What was that knocking, heavy like a diesel engine? Presently he remembered: flying bombs.

"Are we near London, sister?"

"No. This is Brussels. Try to go to sleep."

Everything was dark and the pain had come back at the bottom of his spine. His thoughts ran on in a frenzy. They were out by the bank of the canal, trying to get in the Flails man. They ran forward and picked him up and he had no face.

It hadn't been that way. But the phantasy continued. He was climbing up the bank. There was a row of German faces, and he fired his pistol. Then he went over the top and threw a grenade among a section of Germans launching a raft.

When he awoke, the pillow smelled with the biscuity smell of stale sweat. There was a bottle of yellow liquid tied upside down to a post at the foot of the bed. Every now and then a bubble would rise through the bottle, and he felt a hot stab in his leg.

Later a woman doctor came in. She pulled back the bed-clothes from the cage over his leg and did something with a rubber tube.

"How do you feel?"

"Lousy."

"That's the penicillin. It's doing you good."

"When are you going to cut me up?"

"We've done it."

"Oh."

Next day he felt better. They changed the sheets and the surgeon came. His name was Alexander.

"Here," he said, "souvenirs," and laid some cubes of jagged, crystalline metal on the sheet beside the pillow.

"Is that all?"

"How many do you want?"

"How many did you find?"

"About twenty-five."

He came each day. Always quiet, unruffled, kindly—except once.

Up to then, the ward had been almost empty. In the evening a stretcher was wheeled in and a horribly bandaged figure was placed in a bed at the far end.

"Who is he, sister?"

"A prisoner."

The orderlies went out. The new man lay motionless on his bed. Suddenly the door swung open, and Alexander came in. He was wearing service dress, as if he'd come from a dinner. He was taut with fury.

"Who sent him here, sister?"

"I don't know, sir."

"Have him taken away, do you understand?"

"But I can't, they've taken away the stretcher."

"I don't care. Get him out of here. I won't have Germans in my wards."

A little later, the orderlies reappeared and the German was taken away.

Next morning Alexander was his quiet self. He sat for a moment on the chair by Wilson's bed. "You're coming on fine," he said. "Soon we'll send you to England."

Brussels got on his nerves a bit. The last flying bomb had crashed on a building a few hundred yards away. Then one afternoon the sister came in and gave him a shot in the arm.

"There's an ambulance waiting to take you to the airfield," she said.

The ambulance drove on to the tarmac. And there in the drizzling rain were two middle-aged English women in Red Cross uniforms to hand out tea and a bag of biscuits. They looked like the ones he'd known in Bayeux. They even gave him a packet of American cigarettes.

The plane's engines were revving up. They were bouncing over the runway. From the small window beside his pillow, he watched the dwindling airfield, brown and streaked with water. Then they were swallowed in a cloud.

A W.A.A.F. nursing orderly bent over him, tucking in the blankets.

"Anything you want?"

"No thank you; not a thing."

Out beyond the window, above the tumbled cloud carpet, a flight of Tempests was darting north-eastwards. He thought of the squadron in the salient, of Duffy enthroned in the Mess, Randall with his petrol cooker. What were they doing now? Did they do the attack after all?

He must have slept a little. The clouds were breaking up. Presently in a gap he saw the sea; grey, at first, and ribbed with little white horses, then slowly changing to a muddy colour. Suddenly a line of sand swept beneath; after it grass, vividly green in a shaft of afternoon sunlight; red-brick houses; the darker green of woods.

They went far after that; it must have been deep in the West country. Then the aircraft touched down and the doors were opened. Outside it was mild and a little sad— the eternal English afternoon, when the rain has stopped and the sun looks out weakly before setting.

They lay for a long time in a hut, waiting for ambulances to take them to the train.

The man on the stretcher next to Wilson's was getting restive. He was an old man, far too old for the war: Wilson wondered how he'd got there.

"I live just down the road," he said. "Why can't I go home?"

A W.A.A.F. came up.

"Look, Miss, I live just down the road. Can't I go now?"

Suddenly he threw off the blanket. A party of airmen rushed over and held him down till a doctor pricked his arm.

A Red Cross woman came up. "Can I send a telegram for you?"

She wrote down his parents' address, and handed him a stick of shaving soap and a razor. He lay there, grasping them stupidly, till a W.A.A.F. came and shaved him.

The train moved slowly through the night, with many halts. No one knew where it was going; or perhaps for some curious war-time reason they weren't allowed to tell. After very many hours, when it seemed to have stopped for ever, the doors were opened and stretcher-bearers came in. A little way off, in the moonlight, he saw the rails of a race-track.

"Tattenham corner," said someone, and he was being wheeled down a long brick corridor, into a lift, through wards of sleeping men, into a small room with a hard light high in the ceiling.

After three or four days his parents came. They stood there at the door, looking lost and surprised. His mother came forward, trying vainly, as always, not to cry; and then his father, a little behind, awkwardly holding out his hand.

For a moment they couldn't say anything; and then when they spoke it was all small talk. Just before they left, his mother asked him how it happened. He tried to tell her, he could see her trying unsuccessfully to visualise it. His father just nodded: he had been through it all himself.

At the last moment they remembered the things they had brought, cigarettes and books and a cake. He kissed his mother goodbye and shook his father's hand again. It was time for the afternoon dressing.

When they had gone, it seemed an anti-climax for a re-union which had depended, time and again, on the margin of a second, a few degrees error of some bullet, the chance decision which put someone else, and not him, on the run where the eighty-eight was.

It was an old Victorian hospital, all coal fires and polished brass door handles; but there was a solid air of orderliness and comfort. When the dressings became easier, they moved him out of the private room into a ward. There were four-teen officers in the ward. They were a friendly community; those who could go out came asking for shopping orders, and almost every day someone got a parcel of cake or cigarettes and shared it round the room.

Wilson noticed that everyone at home was much better informed about the war than he was. Even the crude little maps in the newspapers could tell you things you had not realised before: the size of the North-Western Pocket, the the depth of the American thrust towards Aachen. It was curious to know that after the battle for the Channel ports, St. Nazaire still held out—and the Channel Islands.

At first he spent much of his time reading papers, but at intervals he would lie back, closing his eyes and listening to the various activities which went on around him. Then, when he was allowed to sit up by the fire in his dressing-gown, he played draughts and ludo and all the nursery games which are part of a military hospital's equipment. Across every game, people would talk freely about their own particular war. The war, however, was nearly always Normandy, to which no one would go back; seldom Holland, to which a number quite obviously would.

Soon he was able to dress. It was not a month since he'd arrived in England. But, as someone said, that was the trouble with penicillin. The first day he was allowed to go out to the town, he stood at the gate of the hospital, leaning on his stick and looking at the December afternoon. He saw it and felt it with a pleasure he'd never known before: the piled leaves, the reek of a bonfire in the grounds, the cold, clean softness of the air.

A bus came, and there was the simple, commonplace pleasure of getting into it, sitting on the plush seat, holding out a coin for the fare. But the girl wouldn't take the fare. No one wanted to take your money in Epsom—not even the cashiers in the cinemas.

One afternoon he went to a cinema and sat through the newsreel, waiting for the film to begin. There were the usual war shots; the bombs dropping from an aircraft; the smiling crews as they came in to report; the Queen talking with wounded back from Holland.

Presently the pictures switched to somewhere in the East —an island in the Pacific. The Americans were going in with flame-throwers. You saw a figure run out of a bunker. The flame went after him and caught him. It ran through his clothing, till it streamed from his head and limbs. He stumbled once or twice and the flame caught him a second time and he collapsed in an agonised burning heap. Everybody clapped and cheered. Then the newsreel ended, the lights went up, and Wilson looked at the faces of the people round him—kind, friendly, everyday English faces.

Two weeks before Christmas they sent him home. He had looked forward to this homecoming for many days. He had done what he could to see the worst in war and now he was going to enjoy all the things which he'd had to check himself from thinking about in Normandy and Holland.

He didn't tell anyone when he was coming. When the train came into the darkened station, he left his luggage and walked home alone through the town.

He had found a sudden pleasure in walking, especially at night down pavements where there were no mines. Now there was another pleasure, because all the way home familiar objects like trees and shop-fronts and street names came looming out of the night.

He went through the park. There were some iron posts at the entrance to stop traffic going in; he reached out and touched one, as he used to do when a boy, riding his bicycle through the park. The iron was smooth and cold, and he thought: I can touch it whenever I want now, for a whole life-time.

In the first days at home, all his expectations were fulfilled. In the afternoons he would walk out on the marshes by the sea, where nothing lived except the gulls. The stillness was like the stillness of the marshes near Nijmegen when the guns had stopped. He stood for hours by the sea wall, thinking of nothing, watching the movement of the waves, and it seemed that in all his life there had never been anything so good.

At nights he would lie awake, listening to the rain on the windows. Sometimes he thought of the squadron, camped in some cold, sad field. But always he could turn over in the warm sheets and fall asleep again. It was only in the town he felt uneasy. For people there would greet him as if he were a hero, and he would feel fraudulent, because an accident had put him out of the war by a back door.

Outside the town was the country house where the Swanns lived. John Swann had been Wilson's friend at Sandhurst, and John's parents had welcomed him like their own son. He remembered how two years ago they'd sat in the big drawing-room, with its chintzes and polished oak, waiting for dinner, and John had said: "Don't tell the old man I'm going to the Guards yet; I want to keep it a surprise."

It was taken for granted that whenever Wilson came home on leave he would visit this house. Now it was closed to him. John had been killed and Wilson couldn't remind the Swanns that he himself was still alive.

As he went about, he heard people talking about the war. They talked about what they were fighting for—and it made no sense. Soldiers didn't fight for something. War was something which caught them up. After that it was a closed arena, in which you struggled with yourself and your fear. Soon, when the first sensations of home-coming became blunted, he began to feel lost outside this arena.

One evening he went to the bookshelf and took down the book he loved best—Tacitus' *Agricola*. It belonged to the days at school, when he had dreamed of becoming a great classical scholar. He started to read the tight, polished epigrams. But now they meant nothing.

It was as if the war had absorbed all his spirit, and the only things which had ever been real in his life were those which had been in the arena with him—his troop and the Crocodile flame-thrower.

On Christmas Eve the papers were full of the German offensive in the Ardennes. That afternoon there was a letter from Dunkley, sent on from the hospital. It didn't say if the squadron had done the attack, after all; but there were greetings from everyone in the troop. They'd been taken over by an officer called Carroll.

"What will you do when you're better?" said his mother, as they sat at Christmas dinner.

"Perhaps they'll make me an R.T.O."

"What's that?" she said.

"A Railway Transport Officer—they look after troop movements at the big stations."

All the time he was in a torment of anxiety, wondering if the squadron was in the Ardennes and how long it would take to get back with them.

It was called a rehabilitation unit, but it looked like any other army camp. The lines of black Nissen huts, the cook-houses smoking beneath damp trees, the whitewashed stones, the bored sentries. The mess was one of those dreary cafeteria-like places where you buy a book of tickets for your drinks. The permanent staff sat at separate tables. He looked round for faces he might know, but there were none.

"You'll just sit on your arse here," said a burly lieutenant from the R.T.R.

The morning after he arrived, Wilson reported to the Adjutant.

"You're down to take over a troop," he said.

"I'm what?"

"Yes," said the Adjutant, "until we have a draft to provide."

"When will that be?"

"When they ask for one."

"But, damn it . . ."

Suddenly he was gripped by a nightmare vision of spending the rest of the war in this place, with its gloom and despair, the tickets in the mess, the eternal silence of the trees.

He went to the tank park, where the troop he was assigned to was lighting fires under tank tracks to thaw the frozen mud. In the afternoon, there was a lecture by a major back from Burma. They would find it, said the major, a very different kind of war. Tank commanders were run through by Japanese swordsmen who jumped into the turret. . . .

Three days later, the troop was sent for some range practice on the coast. They spent the day shivering beside the tanks while a vessel was cleared out of the firing area.

At last, after three weeks, a draft was summoned to Catterick Depôt—ten officers including Wilson and the R.T.R. man. There was the night train—the blue lamps; the sleeping, unshaven faces; the change at Darlington.

Snow lay on the moors when they left the train at Richmond and came up to the camp in a truck. It was still very early and he ate breakfast alone in a silent mess.

The draft was leaving Catterick that night. Looking at the soulless, sprawling cantonment, its bleak barracks, the whitewashed coal-dumps, the guardroom where defaulters were parading, he felt an overwhelming elation at the prospect.

Ostende Ville was like Charing Cross Station with the glass blown out. It was still very early and there was no one about. Litter was blowing across the rusty tracks, and the only symbol of organisation was a locked door marked "R.T.O." After a while a draft of other ranks marched in. The captain in charge had no idea when the train would leave. When it appeared, an hour or so later, everybody was surprised.

They embarked in a curious assortment of rolling-stock: six-wheeled Belgian coaches from before the First World War and battered London and North Eastern coaches, which had been shipped across complete with sepia photographs of Clacton and Skegness.

After a while the whole collection moved out at walking pace behind a wheezing locomotive.

In the afternoon they pulled up in the middle of a wind-swept plain, where a cook ladled soup from a Soyer stove. There was no other life until they got to Brussels.

They reported at a barracks on the outskirts. There was no nonsense now about passing through the Delivery squadron. They were to go to their units next morning. Wilson found the R.T.R. man, and they took a tram into Brussels for a last look on life.

At every corner urchins and girls stood offering black-market cigarettes. The windows of cake-shops were packed with gateaux and pastries. In discreetly lit restaurants tail-coated waiters bent over the hors-d'œuvres trolleys.

They walked down the Boulevard Max through a jostling flow of American and British soldiers, most of them with girls, others drunk, others just wandering, lost and amazed in the back-line Babylon.

In a side street girls came up from the shadows. "Exhibition, exhibition . . ." said a little hunchback.

"Don't be had," said the R.T.R. man. "They kid you it's the donkey, and it's only a couple of nudes." They passed him by, looking for a bar.

It appeared as a light behind a curtain. They pushed aside the curtain and went in. Music beat down from an unseen loudspeaker, and a teen-age American had collapsed across the bar.

"Dance?" said a woman. She was large and motherly, with make-up like greasepaint. The R.T.R. man shook his head. They drank some brandy and left. Back on the corner of the Boulevard Max, a round plump figure with a blond Flemish face brushed by, and Wilson saw the R.T.R. man weakening.

The girl brushed by again.

"I'd better leave you to it," said Wilson. "Do you need any money?"

The R.T.R. man shook his head. The woman was coming up for the third time. "Thanks all the same. Shall I see you in the morning?" he asked almost anxiously.

Next moment the girl had the R.T.R. man's arm and they vanished in the crowd.

As the life of the city fell behind him and he walked through the dim, empty streets to the barracks, Wilson felt a growing sense of excitement at the thought that to-morrow he would be with the troop. He tried to imagine how he would greet them, and what they would say. He had never realised the depth of his love for them, a love which sprang so unaccountably from mundane things, which in his absence he had almost forgotten—the shared meal, the silent preparation for battle, the closeness of their bodies in the smoke-filled turret, the jokes and obscenities with which they hid their fear.

Perhaps, after all, this was all the war had to offer— neither pride, nor self-respect, nor glory, nor achievement.

Then, as emotions came crowding in on him, he wondered if somehow his absence had made a difference. Later, and distressingly, he remembered that the troop was now Carroll's. Would he get it back again?

XII

ACROSS THE RHINE

THE regiment was at Eindhoven. They found him a billet for the night with a Dutch doctor's family, and in the morning there was a P.U. van to take him to his squadron at Cleve.

All the way from Nijmegen the country was littered with the carcasses of gliders, which had been dropped to link up with the Arnhem landing. Some of them were breaking up in the weather now, and the torn fabric flapped from the frames. Here and there, beside the empty road, houses had been burnt down or spattered with bullets.

There was nothing to mark the German frontier; or if there was, he missed it. The first he knew of Germany was that they were running into a forest, and that this must be the Reichswald. They passed a burned-out Sherman. The Reichswald fighting was supposed to have been as bad as anything in Normandy. It was easy to believe. All the time as you looked up rides you could see white crosses.

The P.U. swung round a bend, and beside the road was a big notice: "This was the Siegfried Line." Another bend, and from a mocked-up clothes-line fluttered towels, a shirt, a pair of long pants. A second notice: "And this is the washing."

As they approached Cleve, he began to feel almost sick with anticipation.

They passed a group of burned houses and a sign with the blue circle of "C" squadron. It pointed up a side road, where the houses were in ruins, spilling out furniture and woodwork. At the top, in a clearing in the rubble, were Crocodiles. Someone sat on a doorstep smoking a pipe. He looked up, shielding his eyes against the sun. It was Dunkley.

While they walked to the cellar which was Duffy's head-quarters, Dunkley gave him a quick account of all that had happened in the past few weeks. The question whether Wilson would take over his troop again was answered without being asked. Carroll was dead. He'd been killed at Weeze, a few miles down the road.

They went down the stairs and there was Duffy.

"Wilson!" he said. "Am I frigging right or frigging wrong?"

"Frigging right, sir," said Wilson. For a moment Duffy just sat there, grinning and searching Wilson's face with his fierce, small eyes. Then he got up and shouted to his bat-man to bring some whisky.

While they drank he told Wilson how Carroll had been standing up in the turret, trying to back down a narrow street, when a bazooka took the flaps off. "You'd better go and see your troop," he said presently. He looked at Dunkley. "Do they know he's here?"

"No, sir."

"Fine," said Duffy. (He loved surprises.)

The tanks stood outside the troop billet, "Superb" and "Sublime" battered and caked with mud. The replacement —"Supreme"—smelt of grease and new tarpaulins.

Randall was standing at the door of the billet. He was talking with some men who were strangers. He didn't see Wilson at first.

"Hello," said Wilson, trying to make it sound common-place, and Randall looked round. His eyes opened wide. "I don't believe it," he said, coming forward and putting an arm round Wilson's shoulders. They went into the house. "What the hell made you come back?" he asked. Wilson didn't answer. He was supremely happy.

That night the officers were sleeping in Duffy's cellar, which was lit with Tilley lamps and filled with the after-smells of cooking. Wilson had brought a small wireless with him, but the only station it could get was the German station which called itself Arnhem. Between playing music, the woman announcer read passages from letters allegedly found on dead Tommies, full of homesickness and pathetic greetings.

Early in the morning Duffy went off to divisional head-quarters. When he came back the officers gathered in the cellar for an "O" group. It was Wilson's first real look at them. In their faces he now saw weariness and resignation, foreboding and tension, and numerous other emotions, which he hadn't suspected.

Duffy gave his orders. The crossing of the Rhine was going to take a week or two to prepare. Meanwhile the troops would be resting: all except one, which was to do some "trials". He glanced at the subalterns in turn. But since only one of them was fresh from England the choice was obvious. Wilson was to leave next day for a canal near Nijmegen.

He went and told the troop. They knew well enough that the "trials" meant that 14 Troop would be in an early wave of the crossing.

"Always Fourteen," said Randall. There wasn't any bitterness about it. It might even have been a matter of pride. Nevertheless it struck Wilson how all through the

war soldiers must have been arbitrarily thrown into unpleasant jobs because their officer was a little fresher or
keener or more favoured than some other.

The canal ran close to a village, and the trials were
watched all the time by an audience of boys and old men.

Engineers had built a raft of giant pontoons. It had a
small motor which worked on a cable staked into each bank.
At a signal the Crocodiles would drive on to the raft,
which sank almost to the waterline, and ride across the
water.

It soon appeared that the trials were largely for the
benefit of the engineers. For the troop it was a holiday.
They slept in an old dairy and every morning a smiling,
buxom girl would bring them eggs from a farm in return
for tins of sardines.

One day they went some miles away to a mobile bath
unit—a magnificent affair of hissing boilers and canvas
screens. You went through a tent full of steaming showers
and came out into a drying-room, where a fresh set of under-
wear was issued, warm and with a slightly toasted smell.

They were just dressing, when someone shouted "V 2",
and away to the east, beyond the Rhine, there was a zig-
zag trail of vapour in the sky: it climbed up and up, till the
zig-zags narrowed and ended.

The same night, Wilson was standing outside the dairy,
talking with some of the engineers, when a small red
light appeared in the sky. It circled and went away again.
"What's that?" he asked. "Jerry reconnaissance jets," said
one of the sappers. "They're getting very inquisitive lately."

While they were doing the trials, Wilson took stock of
the changes in the troop. The most startling was the arrival
of the Milner twins.

175

They were lean and tough, with a certain steel-like quality which seemed to derive from the fact that they came from Sheffield. They had stayed together through all their service—because, they said defiantly, no C.O. had ever dared to separate them. Carroll had put them in the same tank—one as driver, the other as commander. Wilson wondered how it would work out, and how the other three-fifths of the crew felt about it.

At the end of the week Duffy arrived with some senior officers from Division, and the troop did a demonstration. Everyone was satisfied, and the troop got orders to join the rest of the squadron which was getting ready for the Rhine battle in a pine-wood near Goch.

The wood was a forbidding place, full of notices of un-exploded shells and mines, and now and again people stumbled on unburied German dead. It held sinister associations for the squadron, which had been fighting there a few weeks before, and perhaps it was difficult to forget that it was no longer peopled with enemy.

The first afternoon Dunkley took Wilson over some fields to show him where Carroll was buried. There was a row of plain crosses, with Carroll's name and the names of some other tank soldiers. A little beyond were crosses garlanded with flowers, marked "Unknown German Soldier".

They were coming back. It was nearly dusk and everything was silent. Suddenly there was a twang in the wire of a fence ahead of them, and someone or something stumbled off through the undergrowth.

Dunkley stood tense, with his hand on his pistol.

"Who goes there?" he shouted.

But there was no reply.

"I don't like this place at all, chum."

For the rest of the way he looked anxiously through the trees and bushes, refusing to talk, or answering only "yes" or "no" in the sharp, clipped way which he had when his nerves were frayed.

That evening, as they ate their meal, Wilson remarked to Grundy, who sat next to him, about the flowers on the German graves.

"Yes," said Grundy, "it's a mystery how they get there. No one ever sees a civilian about."

Long before you came near the Rhine you saw the smoke-screen. It stretched along the front without a break; a tall white cloud, two or three hundred feet high, curling at its top like a wave-crest caught in slow motion. It had been drifting for several days, covering the British as they moved to the forming-up areas.

All through the afternoon the squadron made slow progress. The roads were full of infantry-carriers and trucks with heavy bridging equipment. For miles around the country was empty of civilians. Cattle with distended udders were wandering through the fields bellowing in pain. Companies of Pioneers had been sent out to milk them, but thousands went unattended.

About six o'clock they came to a cross-roads where Sherman was waiting to guide them out of the traffic stream. Their road went down a shallow valley where a battery of seven-point-twos lay sheeted with camouflage nets. They harboured in some woods on a hillside. It was very still, a soft spring evening. The Rhine lay a couple of miles away, beyond the crest.

Wilson ate with his crew. They lay down to rest in the dusty soil beside the vehicles. Duffy had called an "O" group for 20.00.

While they lay there, one of the drivers came up with a piece of apparatus with mirrors. It was the spare periscope of an amphibious DD Sherman. The DD's must already have gone down to the river for the assault. Uneasily Wilson watched the creeping darkness.

About half-past seven he could stand it no longer. With Dunkley and Sherrif he walked to Duffy's tent at the top of the hill. Duffy was just coming back from Division. They heard his scout car climbing the track. He got out and went into the tent.

"Well, sir, what's the form?"

He undid the flap of his map-case and handed Wilson a sheaf of aerial photographs. "Here," he said, "that's where you're going across tomorrow."

A moment later there was a shattering roar, which swept through the tent, shaking the canvas.

Everyone stood still. All down the front the guns were firing: the twenty-five pounders, the five-fives, the big seven-point-twos in the dip behind. Duffy couldn't make himself heard any longer. They came out of the tent and stood on the crest.

East and west, as far as they could see, the night was lit with gunfire: it flickered through the trees and flashed on the underside of the clouds. The ground shook ceaselessly, and now and again there was a violent, continuing explosion, like a pack of cards being snapped.

"What's that?" asked Wilson.

"The Canadian rocket launcher," said someone. The next moment his voice was drowned by the Bofors anti-aircraft guns.

After a while they went back to the tent and Duffy made a new attempt to give his orders. The first assault wave was crossing at nine that night; Wilson was to stand by from first light. The rest would be on two hours' notice. They were working on the left flank with a Canadian brigade.

There was a grey light filtering through the trees. The firing had changed completely, and instead of the massed bombardment there was now only a spasmodic shoot on the far side of the hill. His crew were still asleep. He went round shaking them.

Randall stirred, saw where he was, and closed his eyes again.

"Come on," said Wilson irritably, "we're on call now."

It was the same with the rest. He had to shake each one twice. Reluctantly they threw back their blankets and began to roll them up.

Presently the drivers warmed the engines. They ate breakfast, watching the sun come up. It was going to be another fine day. Already the sky was busy with aircraft, and over on the landing strip by the guns a little Auster spotting plane was revving up.

Wilson lit a cigarette and walked up to Duffy's tent, to find out how the first assault had gone.

Duffy was shaving—he'd been at Division all night.

"They're fighting in Rees," he said. "You'll be wanted any moment.

Wilson went back to the troop. The tension was almost unbearable.

As time went by they stood beside the Crocodiles, smoking, drinking tea, making jokes which no one would have laughed at ordinarily, wandering off frequently to the latrine. There was going to be an air-drop at ten; perhaps they'd have to wait till it was over.

About nine-thirty there was a sudden increase of artillery

activity. It was over on the right, on the sector between Rees and Wesel. Then from the south there was the heavy drone of an aircraft.

They went into the open and looked. The upper sky was filled with fighters, buzzing and circling like a swarm of bees. Beneath them were Liberators, and away in the distance Dakotas towing gliders. They came on in an undeflected train towards the sector of the heavy firing.

Suddenly the sky beyond the river was dotted with anti-aircraft bursts, but still the aircraft came on. The first parachutes opened, soon there were hundreds floating down in the sun among the flak puffs.

As the Liberators wheeled off the Dakotas came in. The gliders cast off their towing cables. Two of them tilted and plunged headlong towards the ground. The others began to nose down towards the landing fields.

Just then there was a shout: "You're wanted at the top, sir!"

At the top, Duffy said: "You're going over to contact the infantry. Take the scout car and find a Buffalo troop. I'll send on the tanks after you." He gave him the location of brigade headquarters, which was just inside Rees.

He took the car through the wood and found the road to the crossing-point. The river was hidden by smoke. In the fields by the road guns fired spasmodically and startlingly from behind their camouflage. Somewhere nearby the enemy was mortaring.

He came to a high bank. Some Buffaloes were drawn up —tall, ungainly vehicles, like landing-craft on tank tracks. An officer pointed to one of them. The scout car drove in and a flap closed behind it like a draw-bridge.

A moment later the Buffalo climbed the bank. They dipped into the river and thrust out into the current.

From the roof of the scout car Wilson looked across the water. To the right by Rees his view was masked by drifting gun smoke. Ahead, on the far bank, another long smoke trail was drifting from a burning DD. The sounds of firing came from every side, but the river itself was placid and undisturbed.

It took five or six minutes to cross the 500 yards. The strong current kept swinging them downstream. All through the night the Buffaloes had kept course by radio beam.

When they reached the far bank there were no troops; just the burning DD and taped paths past mine warnings. "Better get out of it quickly, they keep shelling," said the corporal. He lowered the flap and a moment later, with a wave of the hand, he was off into the water again.

Wilson directed the scout car through the fields towards Rees. The town was full of smoke and all the roads were blocked with rubble. He found the brigade headquarters in a big shell-scarred house. The Brigade Commander sat at a table piled with maps. There was a mug of tea and a packet of Sweet Caporals in front of him. Somewhere next door a wireless murmured. Sounds of battle came confusedly through the shuttered windows.

"Crocodiles?" he said. "I guess we can use you up left." He called the Brigade Major. "Get on to the battalion and ask if they'd like some Crocodiles."

Wilson leaned over the table, trying to see a map which was upside down to him. To the south-east, where the air drop had been, the bridgehead was reaching towards Wesel. There was only a pocket of resistance in Rees. But on the left the advance had been small: there was a mass of symbols in red—the enemy's colour.

The Brigade Major came back from the wireless.

"Yes," he said, "they'd like them."

Wilson went back to the river and picked up the troop which had come over on the ferry. Their way lay along another of the white-taped paths, past more knocked-out DD's and a Stuart reconnaissance tank smoking gently on the side of a mine crater.

Presently they reached the ruined farm where the battalion should be. Just as he dismounted he heard shells coming. They screamed in and burst with a roar. Before the smoke cleared there was another batch. It was going to be a "stonk".

Lying on the ground with his cheek in the dust and the smell of the explosive in his nostrils he thought: this is the arena again—this is what I asked for. And suddenly he was shaken with a paroxysm of trembling, such as he'd never known before.

He got up and went through the farm buildings. But the battalion must have gone on. There was only a dead sow in a shell-smashed sty, and its mate forlornly prodding it with its nose.

A jeep came by. He stopped it.

"Where do you want to go?" said the driver.

"Battalion H.Q."

"Long way or short?"

"What's the difference?"

"You'll see." The driver took the short way. He raced the jeep up the side of a dyke. At the top there was a rough road. He was in full view of the enemy.

They'd gone about a hundred yards when a shell exploded in the bank a little ahead.

"Hold tight," shouted the driver, as the jeep crashed over a pot-hole. Next moment there was an explosion behind. The enemy was bracketing.

Wilson calculated the remaining length of the dyke—about four hundred yards. Then suddenly a small scruffy figure appeared at the side of the road. He put down a case of mortar bombs and thumbed a lift.

"For the love of Jesus," said the driver, skidding to a stop.

Solemnly, unhurriedly, the little man put his bombs in the jeep and climbed in.

The driver skidded off again. A moment later there was an explosion more violent than any of the others. Where they had stopped there was a haze of brown dust.

At the end of the dyke was a house full of headquarters people—runners, signallers, stretcher-bearers and orderlies.

He pushed through the crowd, asking for the C.O.

"He's gone back to Brigade. Better see the Second-in-Command," said someone.

The Second-in-Command opened his map and pointed to their location. All around the ground was broken by ditches. The enemy held some straggling buildings a few hundred yards northward. "We've got a company tapping out," he said. "There's some armour up there, maybe a couple of S.P.s. Better wait around."

Wilson sat down and waited. Other people were sitting on the floor, some asleep, some drinking tea and smoking. Every now and then stretcher-bearers came in with the air of men coming in from a storm, spat, and sat against the wall with hunched shoulders.

In the afternoon the Second-in-Command was called to the eighteen set. Something was happening at last. He came and told Wilson: "Go and bring your Crocodiles up—we're going to do an attack."

"Pressured up?"

"Yes."

He brought up the troop. They had been kept waiting too long. He could see they were all on edge, particularly the sergeant. He left them pressuring up and ran into the headquarters to get his orders. Everyone was rushing about, but still there was no C.O.

"When's Zero?" he asked.

It wasn't known yet.

Watching time go by, Wilson himself began to feel on edge. In an hour it would be dark.

All at once there were voices in the doorway, and the C.O. came in—a man of about fifty, tired and rather harassed. He spoke for a moment with the Second-in-Command and went through to the eighteen set. Wilson heard him calling the forward company. But now there was no contact with them. The attack was postponed.

Half an hour later Wilson went out to the tanks. It was almost dark; he could just read the gauges. "Supreme" was losing pressure.

The sergeant leaned out of the turret.

"We're not going in in the dark, are we?"

At half-past eight there was a sudden outburst of firing and a clank of tank tracks. He ran out through the back entrance. In the darkness he could see the Crocodiles swinging round. They moved back into the cover of the house and stopped with their guns facing rear.

He ran over to the sergeant.

"What's up?"

"There's an S.P. shooting."

"All right; keep against the dyke."

He called for a torch and went round the trailers again, shading the light with his hands. The pressure of all but one was down to the mark where the flame-guns could no longer work. He went back to the C.O.

"I'm sorry," he said. "I'll have to blow down now."

They pulled back to spend the night by the river. When he had posted the sentries, he stretched out with his face against the fresh, spring-smelling earth.

All night Luftwaffe planes kept bombing and machine-gunning the ferry points. The crews lay on their stomachs, trying to pick out the sounds of British night fighters, till one by one they fell asleep.

In the morning a mist hung over the meadows, blanketing the occasional thud of a gun. Duffy sent over more nitrogen bottles and the troop went back to the battalion. They spent the morning in a patch of scrub, shooting at the buildings held by the enemy. Then the infantry advanced a little and the C.O. called an "O" group.

"We've got the road," he said. "Now we're taking the wood beyond. Crocodiles contact 'B' company. Zero in twenty minutes."

Wilson ran back to the troop and gave the order to move. "Supreme" lurched forward through the scrub towards the buildings where the company was. For one moment the low hull of an S.P. loomed up, and he felt a paralysis across the shoulders. Then he saw the fire-reddened plates above the engine: it had been knocked out.

He had only a vague idea which of the buildings was company headquarters. Some of them were burning and the place was full of smoke. He pushed on, looking for infantry, till he found two privates crouching in a ditch.

"Where's 'B' company?"

They pointed up the road, where shells were exploding.

"I'll take you," said one of them.

Wilson jumped down and ran behind the private through the gardens of some cottages.

185

The shelling was very heavy. It was impossible to detect the shriek of the shell which came near you, so that they exploded without warning. Once or twice Wilson and the private fell pointlessly to the ground as a fireball blossomed and the explosion clapped their ears.

They reached the last of the gardens.

"That's it," said the private, panting.

The door of the cottage stood open, five or ten yards away. Wilson ran towards it.

Suddenly the cottage seemed to bulge outwards.

He had a sensation of redness and of overwhelming noise —noise like a wall of water breaking over him, flattening him and sucking away his breath. He hit the ground. His ears were full of singing. Everywhere there was the stench of brick dust and burnt explosive.

Someone ran past him, into the rubble and the sagging doorway. Wilson scrambled after him, in a dream-world of half deafness.

There were men on the floor, utterly still, their bodies covered with white dust. Crushed by a fan of fallen roof-beams someone was moaning like a child. It was the Company Commander.

"Who are you?" shouted the man who had run past; he was a lieutenant.

"Crocodiles," said Wilson. "We're supposed to be going in with you."

"All right," said the lieutenant. "We're just starting. Follow the leading platoons and if there's any trouble go ahead and deal with it."

The attack went in. The infantry lost a number of men from the shelling, but there were no anti-tank guns and no targets for flame throwers. When it was over Wilson brought the troop back to the road and found Barber in a scout car. He had come across the river to take them to another part of the front.

That night they went to a place about six miles from Rees. In the morning Barber took Wilson to the headquarters of the battalion they were going to work with. It was a little house with an unexpectedly neat garden in the middle of farmland.

"Where's the Adjutant?" said Barber.

An orderly went to fetch him.

As the Adjutant came through the door, Wilson, recognising him, had a sudden impulse to cry out. He came forward and shook Barber's hand. "The C.O. will be free in a minute," he said. Then he turned to Wilson and said as quietly: "Didn't we last meet in the middle of the Peloponnesian War?"

Wilson could hardly answer. He saw Gorman as he had known him an age ago, the Classics master in the Forrens classroom correcting Greek Unseens.

"Yes," he said at last. "About the sack of Melos, I think."

When Gorman had shown Barber into the C.O.'s office, he came back and they walked into the garden.

"What have you been doing since the sack of Melos?"

Wilson started to tell him—leaving school, a year in the Young Soldiers' Battalion, Sandhurst . . . But suddenly the series of events seemed unable to bridge the gap. This wasn't the Gorman he had known; and Wilson wasn't the schoolboy who had given in his Greek Unseen to be corrected. He changed the subject. Automatically they began talking shop—about the extension of the bridgehead and the action to come.

Barber came out, buttoning up his map case.

"Sorry, we've got to be off," he said.

They shook hands. As Wilson climbed into the scout car, Gorman waved. "You're working with the best battalion in the Division," he said with a grin.

"And you're using the best Crocodile troop in the Second Army," shouted Wilson.

It summed up everything that connected them now.

On the way back, Barber told Wilson about the operation they were going to do. The enemy was holding a big cutting in the ground, marked on the map as "unfinished autobahn". The infantry battalion and a squadron of Shermans were going to assault it. When it was taken, some AVREs would lay fascines, and the Crocodiles would go across and flame the next enemy position in a village about half a mile beyond.

Wilson briefed the crews, and in the afternoon they drove out to the place where they were to wait with the AVREs while the infantry and Shermans carried out Phase One. The AVREs were already there. It was a vast meadow, and the enemy was mortaring it methodically, yard by yard.

The attack began at sixteen hundred; but it was soon clear from the calls which flew across the wireless that it was going badly. The enemy had expected it. The Shermans had run into eighty-eights, and the infantry were pinned down by Spandaus. Back in the Crocodiles' waiting area, the mortaring never ceased. A bomb had hit one of the AVRE's fascines. It started to burn like a giant bonfire, angry and red against the cloud-darkened sky.

Just before nightfall the Crocodiles were ordered to pressure up and come forward to help. Then, just as they were running on to the battlefield, the action was suddenly stopped. They were ordered into a little copse, covering the infantry's flank, while Brigade made a new plan of attack.

In the darkness, Barber brought the new plan from brigade headquarters. There was going to be a night attack with Kangaroos.

Kangaroos were old tanks with their turrets removed to make space for carrying infantry. They advanced under fire with the infantry crouched inside; then, when they neared the objective, the infantry jumped out and attacked on foot.

Zero was at twenty-one hundred. At half-past eight he heard the Kangaroos down the road behind him, where they were taking a couple of companies aboard. He lit a cigarette and waited. The artillery opened up, the hand of his watch reached zero. Behind the barrage the Kangaroos must be jerking forward into no-man's-land with their big noisy engines. Lifting one of the headphones from his ear he tried to catch the sounds outside. A minute or two passed, and machine-guns started up.

A Sherman troop came on the air and said the Kangaroos were almost at the autobahn.

The operator leaned over from his hatch. "It looks as if they'll make it," he said.

Next moment there was an outburst of noise and a sudden confusion of messages. Every station was shouting "Bazookas". Kangaroos were being hit one after another. A Sherman was alight. From out in the darkness came a clash of Brens and Brownings and Spandaus. When the noise at last died down, and situation reports came through, it appeared that the infantry had got one side of the autobahn with the Germans still clinging to the other. Phase Two was to wait until morning.

All through the night the Crocodiles stayed on guard

because of the danger of a counter-attack. Inside the turret, with the hum of the wireless and the lamps gleaming dully on the steel of the breech-block, Wilson tried hard to keep awake. Outside there was utter silence and darkness. Shadows, which might have been trees or men, seemed sometimes to be advancing, sometimes retreating. From time to time he got out and walked round the tanks.

Then at first light Barber came on the air, telling them to come back for more bottles.

The air blew cold and damp as they rolled down the road to the rendezvous. Gun crews stood in their pits drinking tea. The cold air, the effect of all the delays, the weariness from lost sleep, made everything seem unreal.

At the rendezvous the other troops were drawn up; they'd come over the river during the night.

"What's going on?" said Sherrif. "Have you flamed yet?"

Wilson shook his head.

Dunkley came over.

"Hear that, Peter?" said Sherrif. "They haven't flamed."

Just then Barber drove up in his scout car. "Hurry up," he shouted. "The infantry are attacking the village."

While the crews were putting in the bottles, the water-truck driver thrust mail into their hands. Wilson had two letters which he pushed unread into the pocket of his map-case.

The way back to the battle seemed very short. They followed the path which the Kangaroos had taken. Then they climbed a bank of excavated earth from the autobahn, and all at once the landscape was littered with dead and burnt-out vehicles. A few feet in front of a knocked-out Kangaroo lay a dead German, still gripping the discharger rod of a Panzerfaust.

They rolled down a slope towards a ruined farmhouse, where a company was already moving off to the attack with trailed rifles. He ran his troop between some outbuildings and jumped down. German dead lay everywhere, some of them crushed by his own tank tracks.

There was a moment's vision of the C.O.—a tall rosy-cheeked man who might have been a farmer.

" Crocodiles, sir!"

He looked round. "Where have you been?"

"Getting new bottles."

The C.O. gave his orders. There was some open ground, a thousand yards long by about three hundred across. On the left was a long wood; on the right a kind of smallholding ending in an orchard. The village lay at the far end. The infantry were going up on the flanks, using the cover of the trees. The Crocodiles were to keep level with them. Then a hundred yards from the village they were to go in and flame. There was a troop of Shermans in the orchard to shoot them in.

Wilson ran back to the troop, and told the sergeant and corporal what was happening.

The tanks were already pressured up.

In the turrets the gunners and operators were in their places. The shells in the racks had their clips off. The red light glowed on the seventy-five firing circuit. The driver let out the clutch and "Supreme" surged forward into the open.

As the troop broke cover Wilson had a clear view of the the village. It seemed far away. The run was going to take four or five minutes.

"Item Four Able, Item Four Baker . . . Line abreast."

The sergeant and corporal swung out from behind and took up their stations on either side of him. They still had their hatches open and he could see their heads bent over the microphones.

They crossed a ditch and the mortaring started. Out on the left, Wilson watched the infantry advancing, dodging the bursting shells. A little ahead in the orchard he could see the olive-khaki Shermans, the tracer of their guns leaping towards the village like red darts. Time to get his own guns going.

"Co-ax seven hundred . . ." The Besa roared into life. Through the smoke and noise of the gun Wilson watched the village come towards him, gaining depth and detail.

The ground rolled out before him, green and flat and clear. Then, without warning, the ridiculous happened. Suddenly the soil wasn't firm any longer. The driver slammed down into first gear. But it was no good. The tank began sinking, clawing at the bog. It tilted a little, sucked and surged, and stopped.

The sergeant's tank bogged as well. Only Corporal Milner escaped. They were six hundred yards from the objective. He called Milner on the wireless and told him to exchange tanks.

As Wilson ran across to "Superb", the ground squelched under his feet. The air was full of explosions. Milner, passing him, grinned and gave a thumbs-up sign.

Putting on Milner's still warm headset, Wilson thought: There's only one way now. He pulled down the turret flaps and ordered: Advance Full Speed.

Beyond the orchard the ground spread wide and flat. He had a sense of nakedness. Suddenly the front of the village crackled with fire. Something slammed into the ground beside the Crocodile. He felt a curious sense of detachment.

A seventy-five fired from behind; the rushing shell skimmed his turret and exploded with a flash on a small red building on the left. He remembered that it was Milner's brother driving this tank, and he thought: Milner's going to devastate this village.

Other shots slammed past. The Crocodile was moving fast—twelve or thirteen miles per hour. All the time he kept searching the ground in front for the watery greenness of bog or the tell-tale circles of yellowing grass, which meant mines.

They crossed a road—a gravel track which went from the orchard to the left edge of the village. He'd been sure there'd be mines there, but there weren't. The ground beyond was firmer. Three hundred yards to go. He picked up the microphone. "Prepare to flame." He hadn't done this since 'sHertogenbosch.

He came in on the left. Suddenly the enemy had stopped firing. There was nothing to show where he was any longer. He set the Crocodile at a building like a barn. The distance closed, and he waited for the panzerfausts.

Something exploded immediately in front of him.

"Flame gun, fire!"

The yellow rod, the slapping fuel. The flame leapt out, roaring and rolling towards the barn. Were there enemy behind it? He didn't know. But the enemy was somewhere. The Crocodile closed in. "Up!" he shouted. The flame lifted for a moment, cascading on the roof.

Another explosion. Fifteen yards from the barn the Crocodile swung round, flinging great clods of earth from its tracks. Walls, gardens, fences rolled past the periscope. The tank straightened up. A cottage stood ahead with shuttered windows.

"Flame!"

193

Again the slapping of the gun, the roar and spread of burning fuel.

One after another, buildings swept into the path of the flame as the Crocodile ran down the face of the village. There was no time to stop and no time to choose targets.

Down in the driving compartment, Milner kept wrenching his steering-bar, trying to throw the panzerfausts off aim. At the end of the village they had to turn. Suddenly there was a clatter from the bogies. Wilson felt a sudden helplessness. "Not now," he prayed; "not a track off now!"—as if God, in his impartial love of armies, could care also for flame-throwers. A few seconds later the track slipped into place again.

They started on a second run. Some buildings were not on fire yet and he looked for places where the enemy might still be hiding. There was a wooden shed. As the flame hit it, the wood blew away in a burning mass, and there in the wreckage was the body of a Spandau.

He looked for more. Suddenly he was seized by the same unfeeling madness which he had experienced long ago at Rosmalen.

As the tank turned for the third run, the Besa jammed. The gunner reached for the cocking-handle, trying vainly to clear it. He stood there steadying himself against the lurching of the tank, sweating over the opened mechanism

"Leave it," shouted Wilson. "Go on seventy-five H.E."

The gunner gripped his trigger. Swinging the turret down the front of the burning village, he began firing off the seventy-five at point-blank range.

He came up for the fourth run. Where, oh where, were the infantry? As always in action, he had lost all count of time. Wherever he swung the cupola, he saw fire and smoke and the track of destruction. But the flame was beginning to fall short and the rack of seventy-five rounds was almost empty.

Then all at once it was over. By the barn a little group of grey-clad Germans appeared, without helmets or weapons, waving a sheet on a pole.

He gave the order to stop firing and opened the hatches. The air was full of smuts and the sickly sweet smell of fuel. He made a sign for the Germans to come out into the open. They moved slowly. At first there were ten; then there were thirty or forty. Wilson circled round them, making a sign towards the rear.

In the hush of the moment he felt a great elation: if ordered, he could have driven through the smoking village and right on to the enemy's divisional headquarters. Nothing could have stopped him; he couldn't be harmed.

Then the infantry came swarming into the village, dodging the mortar shells which the enemy had started dropping now. In the confusion, the Germans began to bring out their wounded, blinded and burned, roughly bandaged beneath their charred uniforms. Some of them looked at the Crocodile. What were they thinking?

He went back to refuel. At the rendezvous point he remembered his letters. One was from his mother. It said: "We are proud of you."

XIII

ARNHEM EPILOGUE

FROM every side of the bridgehead the British and Canadian armies were spreading out in their drive for the North German plain. The evening after the action in the village, Wilson slept exhausted in a derelict cottage. In the night he thought he had a dream that an officer from headquarters was giving him orders. It was a mad dream. They were going to attack some place.

When he woke in the morning the sun beat through a broken window shutter. The officer was in the room. "It was cancelled," he said. "I told the sentry to let you sleep on."

"What was cancelled?" asked Wilson.

"The attack."

That afternoon the whole squadron was transferred to the Canadian army, which was pushing westwards from Emmerich to take Arnhem.

They entered Arnhem by a long Bailey bridge a few days later. To the south were the spans of the great steel bridge which the Parachute Brigade had fought so hard to hold. The town itself was still being shelled. Everywhere there was damage from the new battle and the old, and curiously out of place were streets of small neat houses, basking quietly in the afternoon sunshine.

They cooked a meal on the pavement, wondering what was going to happen. Then orders came for the various

196

troops to join up with columns, which were going to push out to the west in the morning.

Wilson's column moved off at first light. First some Flails, then the Crocodiles, then an armoured bulldozer. Infantry rode on the tanks with cocked Bren guns.

At first, as the column rounded each corner, they waited for the rip of a Spandau or the slam of an anti-tank gun. Sometimes there was something sinister about a house—a slit in the wall or a sandbagged window; and before they went on they would fire at it.

Then the constant precaution became a strain. Soon they slowed only when the road was blocked by mines or tree-trunks, and the Flails or the bulldozer would go forward and clear a way.

They rolled down country lanes, through gentle, wooded hills. Everything smelled of spring—and all about lay relics of the fight of the First Airborne Division. In seven months no one had disturbed them. It was like entering an ancient tomb. Parachutes hung from the trees. Containers lay open where they had fallen to the ground.

At one place they came on a burnt-out jeep. At another the wreck of a British six-pounder anti-tank gun; beside it was a pile of empty shell-cases and a group of wooden crosses. Before they died the gunners had scored an epic victory. Across the road were two old French "Char B" tanks, used by the Dutch S.S. Both had been knocked out by the same shot.

By late afternoon the column had covered ten or twelve miles. Then Barber arrived and told them that the Germans had blown the dykes on the Zuider Zee. The advance had been called off.

Next day they joined a division which was pushing north-wards. Already the war had an air of unreality. In the next few days it became a contest, not with the enemy, but with the worn-out engines of the tanks. Back in England the life of a Churchill had been nine hundred miles. When they crossed the Rhine, the Crocodiles had done twice that mileage. Now, as Zutphen, Coevorden and Meppen were passed they were covering up to forty miles a day.

The crews spent their night halts greasing worn bearings and sealing up oil leaks. On their marches through the day they watched the gleaming squadrons of Fortresses and Liberators which passed overhead on their way to bomb targets beyond the Elbe. One afternoon as they waited in a wood near Meppen, Duffy came up from Division and told them about the great dash of the Guards Tank Brigade to Bremen. The war was ending. It became increasingly hard to think of going into action again.

Then, on the last day of April, the squadron had orders to go to a place near Oldenburg, where an enemy battle group was holding out. The squadron waited in a field under mortar fire. Towards the town a great column of smoke was rising from a burning dump. The enemy commanded a road about half a mile away. There was supposed to be an S.P. somewhere and it was going to rain.

Barber wirelessed Wilson to pressure up and take his troop forward.

As they went up the lane towards the enemy, he thought how dismal it would be to be killed when the war was so nearly over, when nothing one did or failed to do would in any way affect the outcome.

As they came up to the enemy's position some twenty-five pounders opened fire. The shells crashed into a sombre house against a dark wood. Suddenly a group of figures appeared from the back of it running for the cover of the trees. In an instant every machine-gun opened fire on them. When it was over, there was no need for Crocodiles.

They formed up with a column and began to move along the road towards the town. That night the infantry patrolling through the woods found the line held by Alsatian dogs tied to trees.

For two days the squadron harboured in a chicken farm. The farmer and his wife and two daughters lived in a little room. There was no contact with them, because it was forbidden to fraternise with Germans.

On the last morning, as the troop was getting ready to leave, the old man came to Wilson weeping. In his hands were his sporting guns; fine old guns, with beautifully chased barrels. Presently he managed to make Wilson understand. He'd been told he would have to surrender the guns to the military government.

Wilson was embarrassed and in a hurry. He pointed to the ground and made the motions of digging. Suddenly the old man's face cleared. He spoke volubly and gratefully, and tugged at Wilson's sleeve.

"Well, what is it?" said Wilson impatiently.

The old man led him to the lane where the Crocodiles were parked ready to move off. A few yards in front of "Supreme" he bent down to brush away some leaves, and there, in the earth, you could see the circular cuts where the enemy had left teller-mines.

In the last forty-eight hours, the war became a phantasy. On the last night but one, Wilson was awakened by one of his sentries. He had captured a German soldier stumbling about at the end of the tank-line. Wilson shone a torch on the man, who wore the uniform of a sergeant-major.

"What are you doing? Where do you come from?" he asked.

Immediately the sergeant-major began a loud protest. From his pocket he produced a slip of paper. He was on leave, he said, and no one could take him prisoner.

Next morning they were two miles from Oldenburg, waiting at the side of the road, when a lone Lancaster bomber appeared overhead, circled the town and dropped a bomb. Someone had heard on the wireless that Hitler had killed himself in the bunker in Berlin. There were rumours that the German High Command was surrendering.

Soon after dark, when the squadron was still stationary, Barber sent Wilson back to brigade headquarters to find out what was happening. All along the road the infantry transport was travelling with full lights on. But Brigade had nothing to tell.

They entered Oldenburg the next morning. Some of the shops were open and all the beer houses. About four in the afternoon Wilson's troop reached the river by a half demolished bridge. The streets were full of transport and infantry. In all the confusion a German officer rode by with his wife and family in an open car.

Barber told him to put the Crocodiles in a position covering the bridge. As they were fixing the arcs of fire, Barber's driver came over from the scout car. "It's over," he said. "Cease fire at 0800 hours tomorrow." Wilson told the crews. They finished manoeuvring the tanks into position and made some tea.

Six years' war didn't end neatly. On the night of the cease-fire the Canadians went mad with the madness of men who fought a campaign with three hundred per cent casualties. Unerringly they found the larger wine cellars, and when these were put under guard they found others. In an orgy of relief they began to throw grenades and fire off rifles and machine-guns in the streets. To walk through Oldenburg on the night of May the Fourth, 1945, was as perilous as anything since D-Day.

Two nights later the squadron had a party. Duffy had sent one of his new lieutenants to scour the countryside for whatever liquor the Canadians had left. There was no wine. But the lieutenant returned from Bremen with two large barrels of beer and a canister of liquid which was later identified as part of the propellant for a V2 rocket. It was a great party. It started at seven and at half-past eight Wilson drove the last of the unconscious to the first-aid post. At six next morning—VE day—they began the road march to a place where the regiment was concentrating.

As they drove along the road to Delmenhorst, it occurred to Wilson that this was their last operation as a squadron. He felt apprehensive at the thought of returning to normality: a vision rose before him of offices with "In" and "Out" trays, training programmes, dinner nights in mess, fatigues for the men and dismal queues at the cook-house.

He looked round the tank. Down in front Randall had his flaps closed, recovering from the party. The operator sat huddled in his hatch. The gunner, as always, was asleep against Wilson's legs.

In the afternoon Barber appeared in a scout car and halted them. Wilson's worst fears were fulfilled. A little way ahead across the fields were the walls of a barracks. One by one the troops were called forward through the gates and on to the square where the tanks of the other squadrons were already assembled in long straight rows.

The R.S.M. was there to guide them. "Left a bit, sir—

two foot forward—back six inches. That'll do, sir. We'll get a white line drawn tomorrow."

There was something unnatural about it—the rows of tanks beneath the grim walls of the barrack blocks still painted with Nazi slogans. It was untactical; even though the war was over you kept thinking: "What'll happen if there's an attack? They'll never get out."

A truck came round with petrol. While they refuelled, Wilson went to look at the rooms the troop had been given. All the way he kept seeing strange officers—they seemed to be sharing the barracks with another regiment. And then he realised: they were from the other squadrons.

Perhaps unconsciously he'd been thinking of finding the regiment as he'd last seen it together—at Ashford, fourteen months ago. He'd been thinking of Harvey and Benzecry, Dean and Argentine, and William Home and Waddell. The thought of them had softened the prospect of returning to live in mess a little.

Back on the square, the crew looked across at each other and then at the little hoard of illicit rations they'd unloaded from the tank—sugar and steak-and-kidney pudding and margarine and milk.

"Shall we take it to the room?" said the driver.

"You can't hide that lot," said Randall.

They looked at Wilson. "Put it in the turret," he said; "you never know; we may still need it."

But as he watched them march away, awkwardly bent with their blankets under their arms and their mess tins clattering by their sides, Wilson knew that it was over. It ended for different people at different times, and for him it had ended at the end.